I am Finally Me

I LEARNED TO LET GO AND I SET MYSELF FREE

By Rita Owen

All the information contained in this book is based on the life experiences and opinions perceived and expressed by the author.

No part of this book may be reproduced or transmitted in any form or by any means electronically or mechanically, including photocopying or recording without prior written consent by the author or the publisher.

This book is printed in the United States.

Publisher:

Rose Gold Publishing, LLC

www.rosegoldpublishingllc.com

Copyright@ 2019 Rita Owen - All rights reserved.

ISBN-13: 978-1-7332638-6-3
ISBN-10: 1-7332638-6-1

I am Finally Me

I LEARNED TO LET GO AND I SET MYSELF FREE

By Rita Owen

Table of Contents

The Burden ………………………..……………….............1

The Eavesdropper……………………… ....…….………..5

Insecurity……………………………….......………..….…..9

Fear…………………………….........………………….17

Time Wasters…………………… ....…………………… 29

Getting Trapped …………… .....…………………….36

Being Perfect…………………….........…………..43

Our Perception…………………… .....……………….. 49

The EGO……………………………. ....…………….57

Re-Writing My Past..……………….. .....………………. 63

Forgiving ..…………………………......………..……. 70

Who Am I? ...……………………...……….…… …… 75

Saying NO! ……………………… ....…….………..79

Realization…………………… .....……………….83

Now What? ……………………… ....……………...90

Who Cares…Just Do It!...………………......…………….. 95

v

Dedication

I am dedicating my first book to my son Frankie… Without you, none of this would be possible.

Bringing you into this world showed me I am capable of so much love. You have taught me what true love is and what it means to have a special bond with another human being. You have made every day in my life possible and amazing. Without you, my life would not be where it is today.

I love you Frankie more than words could ever express.

You are my greatest gift and accomplishment.

Acknowledgment

I want to say thank you to my best friend Mary C Knauf
for being the strength when I needed it,
and encouraging me to keep moving forward in my life.

Thank you to Elisa Kehler for helping me in my healing
so I can do what I love.

Thank you to John Murray for sitting down, and wanting
to get to know who I am.
Listening to your story has allowed me to start writing
my story.

Thank you so much!

Introduction

Every day I sit with my journal and write. I have written about how I felt, what has happened in my life, how it all makes me think about what I want to do with my life. I have even written about the types of relationships I want in my life or how they have had gone wrong in my life.

One day, a few years ago, I was writing when I found myself having a conversation with someone or something that was not in front of me. I was getting clarification as to why I was feeling the way I was and how I can help people with what I have learned through my experiences. I could not believe it. At first, I thought I was crazy and just talking to myself, as time went on, everything was making sense. I heard very loudly in my head we are talking, YES this is real, I am your Angel. You are talking to many different Angels who have helped you through your life. This is the way we were able to help you realize you can communicate with us from the other side. Your spiritual gifts are powerful, and it is time for you to start using them.

I couldn't believe it…it took me a little bit to trust what was happening, but it never shut off. I was having conversations with the spirit world to help myself and other people. I was starting to know things I could never have known before. I knew it was real, and my gifts were getting very strong. I was aware my life was changing in a way I never thought was possible.

When I was younger, I was always attracted to psychics and mediums. I always wanted to know if I was on the right path or what was going to happen in my life. Would I ever meet the right guy, have children, and lots of money, you know the drill? They always told me I was not listening, I have my own gifts that I am not using, and I am to be doing this work helping people. I always thought they were crazy. How could I be doing this kind of work? Who am I? I come from a difficult background. I kept dropping out of college to have fun. I was always told I was no good, a drug addict, alcoholic, and selfish. All I cared about was my person. How could I have these gifts? I knew I was different. I knew I was able to understand things before someone else did. However, never in a million years knew I would be where I am right now.

Being able to communicate with Angels the way I do is a fantastic gift. However, one thing about this gift is they are always with me. They see all I do or don't do. They can see when I am spiraling out of control or moving forward. They are always there to help me realize I am better than the not so good behavior patterns I fall into. They are there to tell me to quit fighting with my ex-husband, along with letting me know how to stop trying to fix people. They teach me to let go of what is not my responsibility so I can live powerfully. They also show me that I am amazing because of the way I have changed my life.

Being guided by my Angels has helped me to see different perspectives of every situation I have been in. I get to see the bigger picture of every experience so I can see what I needed to learn and teach. It truly is a fantastic gift. My life has changed in so many great ways because I can communicate with my Angels. Ways in which I never thought was possible. This book is one of the ways that has genuinely changed my life.

On this particular day of Angel Writing, my book title came to me, or I thought it was my book title. "Who Cares…Just Do It" Who Cares, Just Do It…Who Cares, Just Do It… I wrote it over and over again until I realized what my Angels were telling me. It was time to write my book, and it did not matter how it turned out I just needed to do it. I dropped my pen and sat back with a huge smile on my face. I knew it was time, and the Angels were going to help me write what I needed to say.

I have always wanted to share my story, but I did not know how to do it without just talking about all the negative experiences that occurred. I did not want to call out anyone; I just wanted to show no matter what happens to you in life; you can always live powerfully. The Angels have decided I am ready, and they are going to write it with me. I am so grateful for my journey and the gifts I possess.

My wish for you, while reading this book you can look at your own life through my experiences. I wish for you to decide to look at your individual situation differently and start to make great choices for yourself. I want you to climb out of your own mud puddle, dry yourself off, and begin to realize everything that has gone on in your life has actually been for your highest good. This is why it is so important to share with you some of my stories. I want you to stop living your life as if life is happening to you and start living your life as life is happening for you.

Can you imagine when you are done reading this book your whole world will shift? The changes you will make just by reading some of my points of view along with how I have rewritten my own past? That would be the icing on the cake for me. You literally changing everything you thought and turning it into the vast possibility in your life. No matter where you are at in your life, you can always decide something different for yourself.

Helping people has always been my main focus in life, as I can move past my own pain, I can help others. This is why I became a Spiritual Life Coach. I have learned that I can help many people through tough times in their life by sharing my own experiences and channeling from the other side. I have a gift that allows me to know what to say and when to say it, so my clients see a different perspective for themselves. I am always in awe by my work, and how I can really help people who need it. Nothing fills me up more than watching someone discover their independence from the story they carry through life.

I hope you enjoy reading this book as much as I enjoyed writing it. My wish for you is to see yourself through my stories and change the way you see your life.

The Burden

For as long as I can remember, I have always tried to be a kind hard working person, keeping the peace and trying to stay out of trouble. Trouble always seemed to find me anyway. Growing up I always thought I was a bad kid, getting yelled at, having my fair share of beatings, never hearing anything positive about myself. I always felt like I was being punished for being alive.

I have spent so much of my life trying to be the best at whatever I did so I can make people proud of me, or accept me. I thought to be accepted I needed to do something great in my life. I had to have a great job and raise my child right. That is when I would be accepted. However, that never happened. I never really got the recognition I was so desperately looking for. I have always felt like I brought a significant amount of burden to the people around me. It took a long time for me to realize I am the only one who can truly recognize and approve of myself. If you are looking for the same thing, only you can give yourself the approval you need.

Have you ever just done whatever it took to be accepted by your family, peers, or people you look up to? Did you drive yourself crazy trying to reach a bar that was never to be achieved, only to beat yourself up? I have done this my whole life up until a few years ago. It is exhausting trying to measure up to someone who will never be a part of your life anyway. Even the thought of what people must think of me if by chance they heard all the great things I was doing, or how great I turned out to be would have me spinning my wheels. It's like living in a constant fantasy from my past, pining for the recognition and approval I would never receive. This is what we do to ourselves…I know I am not the only one.

I grew up in a family that was not perfect. No one's family is perfect, but for me, it was tough. Not all the time, however, I have my scars from all the chaos and fighting that ensued. When I was going through my first divorce is when I was introduced to self-development. I was able to realize I grew up in the perfect family to prepare me for my life.

I hated my childhood. I grew up always feeling like I was not good enough, not quite enough, not healthy enough, smart enough, skinny nor pretty enough…literally, nothing was enough. I felt like someone who was a burden and a drain. I lived into that lie for many years until I finally started to really dive into who I truly am. I had to stop being angry and a victim of my childhood so I can eventually climb out of my own mud puddle. One thing about childhood, as kids we take everything so personally, and it will follow us our whole life until finally, we decide we are the ones in control. Most of us won't find that out until later in life when we are so sick and tired of blaming everything that goes wrong in our life on our childhood. Being born into this world, it is all about us for most of our youth if we are lucky. However, that all about us concept can allow us to feel like no matter what happens, it's because of us, or if we have a rough or violent childhood, we keep the anger deep inside of us and blame the world for our complicated life.

Think about it, from the time we are born to the time we start school, everything is about us. Our parents eat, sleep and breathe us. We are always with them, we hear everything, we may not understand it, but we hear much. We also start to think if things are not going well, we believe it's our fault because of what goes on in the home. We can hear our parents fighting, they may say our name, and we automatically think it's about us. There could be a situation they are talking about, and we feel like it is our fault. When we are young, we internalize everything and think it's our fault when it all seems to fall apart.

I was always a sick kid. I could not breathe most of my childhood. I had many hospital stays, and I was on a lot of medicine. It was expensive medicine that drained my parents' bank account to keep me breathing. I remember listening to my parents fight about money and how expensive the hospital bills were and the medicine. I remember feeling so bad and guilty for spending their money and them not having enough money to survive. I always waited until the last minute to let my parents know I needed my prescriptions filled, they should have known, but I always waited to the last minute to remind them. I hated being so sick and needing the medicine that was so expensive. Being such a burden to my family weighed heavy on me, I tried to wait as long as I could, but I always made the situation worse. Up until this past year, I still would wait until the last minute to get my prescriptions filled. Even during both of my marriages I always waited. I did not want to put that upon someone else, even though I needed the medicine. My childhood insecurities continually plagued me, and I hated knowing I was still a burden even in my adulthood. Now that I am on my own, I am learning no matter what it is that I need, it's okay.

Isn't that crazy? I made myself even sicker putting off and stretching my medicine than if I would just have gotten what I needed. I would never deny anyone medicine and yet here I am doing it to myself. Especially my son, I have given and would give him anything he ever needed, I would never make him feel like I felt. Yet I always deny myself. When I look back, I see how I took everything personally, as if I was the cause of all the misfortune in our family.

When you grow up in a household where the money is a significant issue all the time, the kids take on those burdens. Whether or not the parents mean too, it happens, that is why it is so important to let your kids know it's not their fault. Kids will take on any responsibility in the home without you realizing it. Kids also hear almost every conversation nothing really is a secret.

I have lived my son's whole life reversing what I went through. I never wanted him to feel like he was the cause of anything that went on in our home. I worked so hard letting him know, sometimes things are just the way they are. No one is to blame, especially the children.

The Eavesdropper

I remember listening to adult conversations when I was young, conversations that I should not have been listening to. Somehow my mother would always know when I was listening. I could hear her say quit talking and make me leave the room to go do something else.

For as long as I can remember I have always eavesdropped on conversations my parents and everyone else would have. I didn't know what it was about me then. I would hear things I did not or should not have known. I believe this is where I learned to take everything personal. As a child we don't have an understanding of what is really going on. We only hear bits and pieces and we fill in the blanks with our little brains. We turn things inward and take responsibility for everything happening all around us.

I would be watching T.V. and all of a sudden hear my name. Immediately, I was eavesdropping. I was always listening for my name or anything that had to do with me. My parents would always say, I was afraid of missing out on something. No matter what I was doing, I would stop and just listen for whatever I needed to hear.

I remember when we were living in an apartment, my Mother came into our room, I was in kindergarten then, she got my older sister up from bed. I was already awake and wanted to go, but she didn't ask for me to get up. I thought to myself, maybe she thought I was sleeping, but I wasn't. I desperately waited for her to come get me, but she didn't. I could hear the two of them talking, just being with each other. It drove me so crazy, I felt so sorry for myself. She finally came into the room when it was time to get my younger sister and me. I was so angry and sad, I felt then I was not good enough. Maybe she did not love me like my older sister. At that time, I knew I never wanted to miss out again.

It's funny how when things happen in our lives, even when we are very small children. We are smart enough to figure it out, make decisions and learn how to protect ourselves from getting hurt again.

However, when we listen to conversations that are not ours, we start to become paranoid, scared someone is talking about us and we are not measuring up.

A lot of the conversations I would listen to were my mother telling my grandmother and/or my aunt how bad we were, or what it was that we did. For me it was so embarrassing. I hated it…I knew I was not good enough and I would probably never amount to anything when I got older.

It was almost like listening became a way to figure out how I was going to handle a situation or not. Whether, or not I was going to avoid being around someone in the family, because I was so ashamed of whatever it was that I did. Even if it was so stupid, I always felt tremendous shame and regret. I never wanted my face attached to the horrific things I ever did.

When we are young, it's true what they say, children are impressionable. We turn what is said into so many things. We learn to defend ourselves when we may not have to. We learn to be in defense mode all the time. As we get older, we realize how much undoing that needs to be done, because we are constantly sabotaging ourselves. A lot of it stems from our early development. It's not an excuse, it sadly is a fact.

Now, don't get me wrong. I am not blaming my life on my parents...I have grown from that. There was a period of time when I did blame them, I blamed my whole world on them. What I am saying is we need to have self-realization. When we do the things we do, we need to ask ourselves when did it start, how did we learn it? What motivated us to create a defense mechanism for our lives? We all do it, even our parents, and their parents. We are not in this alone. Realizing I had choices in everything that happened in my life, allowed me to see the lessons in everything that occurred.

We are all on the same spinning wheel when it comes to this. It's not that we blame, it's that we are not brave enough to stop the cycle. We do what we've always been taught our whole lives, until one day we are so pissed off we start to do something different, or maybe we walk away.

I walked away from my family 27 years ago. Writing this book allows me to see how much I took personally, and made decisions from my experiences. Now, obviously there is more to that story and I will be sharing bits and pieces of it here in this book and more in my next book "Breaking the Chains from My Past." We make decisions from our experiences and live into those choices.

One of the major things I teach my clients as a Spiritual Life Coach is to look at the bigger picture, not just what's in front of you. There are many sides to a story, as humans we typically only see one side and go with it. Yet, there are different sides to a story we never get the full picture until we experience hindsight. Most times, we are to stubborn to say we are sorry, too much time has passed, or we were not meant to be together for the rest of our lives. Either way, what we learn hinders who we are.

Insecurity

Have you ever noticed how insecure we become the more we eavesdrop or try to really pay attention to a conversation you may think is about you? It does not matter if you are at work, school, or at an event. We are all self-conscious that maybe we are doing something wrong, we are in trouble, or we are not measuring up. It does not matter how old we are…we are still worried and insecure.

It seems we all deal with this in one way or another. Some of us are very good at hiding how we feel, but most are not. The ones, who seem to be good at hiding, eventually have a massive breakdown because of it. I have never been good at hiding my emotions or insecurities. They run deep, and I have worn them as clothing.

I have realized, in my experience of insecurity, if I don't share what needs to be said or what needs to be done, I will try to hide from the situation. I make it much worse for myself then if I would just say what needs to be said. It's almost like living in a snowball that keeps on running down a giant hill that won't quit. It will make me dizzy, tired, and nervous. Most of all, I feel panicked and frustrated. When I get to this point, I start to lash out. I will also try to stay a few steps ahead of everyone else, so I am not found out that I actually don't have it all together.

I know I am not the only one who does this, but when I am in it, I feel entirely alone. I will make my life a living hell. The worst part of it is being in a relationship trying to keep it all together. The insecurity is overwhelming, I always feel like I have to overcompensate just for someone to be with me. When my partner figures it out, it becomes open season on me. I lose the protection I have created for myself, and all hell will break loose. I will be reminded of my short-comings, and it will never end until I end the relationship.

In most relationships both partners have insecurities. However, one is better at hiding than the other. Unfortunately, relationships have a terrible time staying together because of it. We learn to be dishonest in how we are genuinely feeling, and we are so afraid of being found out, we sabotage the relationship. It is possible one person will start to share their feelings and change, while the other will still keep their insecurities to themselves.

This is how my second marriage was. Exactly what I just shared. I married someone whom I thought I was madly in love with and we would be together forever. Before we married my son and I moved into his home. I started to see a side of him I did not like. Although, if I am being candid, I did see some red flags before we moved in. However, I chalked it up to being a family man was new to him, and I gave him a break. As time went on, we were in his house, I saw someone who was not as open as I was. All he shared of himself was how much better he was, nothing ever went wrong in his life until I got there.

I already felt utterly insecure with who I was, because my life was not like his. My whole life was about struggle and abuse. I had to figure out how to stay afloat with my child being the priority. I brought my baggage into this relationship that my partner did not know how to handle. In his defense, he thought life was effortless. He never really had to deal with significant life problems and children. He was all about how to make sure he got what he wanted.

I felt like I owed him. I had baggage and a child. I looked at myself as a huge burden that just made someone else's life a mess. It didn't help; I was reminded of it almost every day. Many lessons were taught to me in this relationship. They always made me feel incredibly insecure and very angry. I was mostly very angry with myself since I brought my son into this relationship. However, there were securities I needed for my son, and I did not think I could give it to him myself. So, I allowed this man to be a part of our life. The old saying goes…when one makes their bed; they have to lie in it. That is the way I saw it. I didn't think I could do it on my own, even though I was already doing it. It was hard, and I wanted so much more for my son.

As I am writing, I see my responsibility in all of this, but I want you to understand, being insecure makes you do things that may not be for your highest good or anyone else around you. I stayed in that relationship for seventeen years. I recently became unmarried, and I am finding some of my insecurities were put upon me by my spouse. I am not as bad as I thought.

I also realized he did have some insecurity at the beginning of our relationship, but I wanted him to realize how amazing of a man he was. I helped him to see his own greatness and that he had so much more to offer then what he could see in himself. I helped him realize he is an extraordinary person; I was forever grateful that he took my son and me on. That was the moment when I gave up any power and any confidence I had inside me. The more time that went on, he started to express how much better he was than us. He would never let me forget what he did for us.

These are a few examples of how we let our insecurities hold us back. We don't do what we really want or need to do because we create a world around us to make sure we stay stuck. Until one day we actually wake up and do something about it. Our insecurities play so much in our lives, especially when we are not even aware of what is happening.

I am for the most part a confident person; however, the insecurities that have been planted in the back of my mind when I was a child have been watered by the experiences in my life. It's like saying, "today is going to be a bad day." You just planted that seed, and what happens? The entire day you watered the seed with all the experiences of a bad day you created for yourself. At the end of the day, you say to yourself, "that was the worst day ever." You created the worst day ever by constantly putting yourself in situations that you perceive as bad, solidified it by saying "of course", "what else can happen", "this is my life", "this always happens to me", you put the intention out there and drew it right to you.

This is what I have done all during my adult life. I have let my childhood experiences dictate how I would live my life. When you feel like you need to be rescued because you are not smart enough or capable to figure out life on your own. I married my first husband because he was perfect for getting me out of my situation at home with my family. My second husband was to help me raise a man. I had been told over and over again, my son needed to be raised by a man, a woman, would not raise a boy properly alone. I believed the lies people told me, all I wanted what was best for my baby.

Isn't that amazing how we do this to ourselves? We don't even realize we are doing it. This is something I had to really come to terms with. Most people would not be responsible for what happens in their lives, they would say this happened to me, it was out of my control. I lived this way for many years. We should start asking ourselves "was it really"?

I have been late for work these past few weeks, I can't seem to get out of the holiday patterns, and winter has given us a run for our money. Yesterday, I was speeding trying to get to work somewhat on time. At this point is when I realized I have been keeping myself late, and everyone in front of me is not in as much of a hurry as I am. I have found myself tailgating lately, now I know I have done this a few times in the past few weeks because some drivers were not very happy about it. They would grab my attention, and I immediately backed off. Never mind the fact I keep leaving later and later, which will guarantee me not to get there on time. With all my might I continue to try. It has become quite a habit until yesterday.

I was driving behind a pick-up truck, I didn't think anything of it, because he was at a speed, I was comfortable at. The next thing I see he has driven to the center of the road. I start to slow down because I wasn't sure what was happening. It was at that time; I see him waving me to keep driving. So, I did. The next thing I saw looking through my rearview mirror was him getting right back on the road. I didn't think much of it. I was grateful I got to pass and keep going. I continued to drive fast to make it to work. There were other people in front of me, but I really didn't think I was right up on the person in front of me. All of a sudden right before eight a.m. my cell phone was ringing, the caller was no one I knew; however, I knew it was the guy behind me. He got pretty close to my car to read my number off my back window. I ignored it, and let it go into voicemail. I decided if he leaves me a message, I will listen to it at work. As I continued on my journey to work, I was so focused on the call and the time was ticking away. I turned down the wrong street and sat at a light. It was five after eight a.m. when I walked quickly into work and took my seat. I work reception at a law firm, so I should be there on time to open the phones for the business.

When I got myself situated, I remembered I had a message waiting for me. Yes, it was the guy behind me leaving me a message to slow down and quit tailgating. At first, I got a little snarky, but then I knew my Angels have been putting cars in front of me on purpose, trying to slow me down but I was not listening…So they made sure I heard their message loud and clear. I listened to the message that he left a few times, and decide to text him a response, so he knew I listened to what he had to say. I felt pretty good when I decided to take responsibility and acknowledge my crazy driving. I thanked him in a text and promised to leave time for myself in the morning, so I would not be in such a hurry. When I left work yesterday, I drove the appropriate speed and even coming into work this morning I was on time and did not tailgate or speed. Although, there was a time or two when I had to realize I was not late, and just enjoy the ride.

I am sitting here thinking to myself, why did you just share this story? My answer is, instead of making myself wrong, insecure or angry. I realized I had a responsibility in this and to see how I keep putting myself in the same situations all the time. This story applies to what I have been sharing with you, and it is so relatable to so many people who do the same thing. I could be so mortified and insecure with the guy leaving me a message because my car and my face are now attached to the bad behavior. Instead, I feel empowered to be responsible for my actions. I actually look forward to seeing the guy again, I am grateful for the wake-up call.

As I shared at the beginning of the book, I can communicate with my Angels. When I ignore them and do what I want, my Angels will always find ways to get me to listen. That driver was my Angels telling me to slow down or else the outcome will not be good. Which means it saved me a lot of drama.

Look at your own life, what are you repeatedly doing and blaming others for making your life miserable? When you begin to get those jolts of WAKE-UP, you start to shift the way you think and see life. Taking responsibility for your own actions actually leaves you feeling empowered in your life.

Fear

When I think about my life and all I have been through, fear is something that comes up for me all the time. I am so afraid of people finding out I don't have it all together. I am scared of asking for help in fear that people will think of me as being stupid or incapable. I am afraid people will talk behind my back and I will look bad to everyone who is in front of me. I am so scared my past will creep up and destroy everything I have been trying to do. I am afraid my son will see me as someone who ruined his life and will hate me. I am so scared I am so damaged that no one will give me the time of day. As I write, I am asking myself, are you feeling sorry for yourself? Is it possible you are finally being honest with yourself with your fears? The truth…I am being honest with myself. I have been terrified of doing everything wrong in my life, most importantly not raising my son right. My son not having respect for me because of everything we have been through and the choices I have made for us to survive.

I remember when I was young, I felt fearless by anger. Isn't that an interesting observation? You might be asking yourself what does fearless by anger mean? It's a made-up term I have created. I was such an angry kid and young adult. I did not really care who or what was ahead of me. Even though I was terrified, my rage would give me the courage I needed to handle any situation. When I think about it, it can be quite a scary concept. Considering the way, I was raised, all I knew was anger that turned into rage. I had this façade about me that people thought I was hardcore, but deep down on the inside, I was a terrified child.

I used the fearless anger mostly with men. I never had a good role model when it came to men. I was taught to be afraid of men by their actions and the way they treated a woman. I grew up in a household where fear plagued our home. When my father was on the rampage, it was terrible. He was violent and ruthless with his words. He would make you feel bad about yourself, so you could never really stand up to him. I hated it, I knew deep down inside of me, I did not deserve what I got. Unfortunately, that was the family I was in. I did not know any better. I attracted men who were like him.

When it came to needing help, I would try to do everything myself. If I had to go to the mechanic, I would act hardcore like I knew what the problem was so I would not be taken advantage of. I always saw my Father in the face of men. I would stand tall, act sharp and let them know, I know what you are trying to do. It's so sad, because not only was I riddled with fear and anger, I did not trust anyone.

When I finally had the nerve to ask for help, I would ask my guy friends who liked me for help. It did not matter whether I liked them or not, they were safe for me. I always trusted the guys I was not interested in. Maybe because they would do anything for me just so I would be with them. I hated using people, but sometimes

I really needed the help, and I didn't want to ask anyone who would hold it over my head.

Growing up in the household I did, I learned not to trust guys who would do things for my Father. Any guy who would bend over backward for him, I would break up with immediately. They were no good to me at that point they would not be able to help me out of my situation. I always felt like he got to them as well and I had no ally.

I realized Fear has plagued me my whole life. I wasn't just afraid of men; it was with people, employers, and my own family. I was so scared to show my true self. I was this little girl desperate to get out of my body and yell to the rooftops I Am Awesome. However, I was taught, it's not polite. You never talk about how great you are or how you did a great job with something. You always kept it to yourself, so you did not hurt anyone else's feelings. I would have been considered vain or boasting about myself. Even my body, it developed so fast, I was so afraid kids would say something my parents thought would be my fault. It's a horrible way to live.

I had my son at twenty-three years old. I was a baby having a baby. That's how I felt, I had no idea about babies and what they needed, how was I going to take care of one? When I had my precious little boy finally in my arms, I was terrified I would not know what he wanted or needed. I was worried about how I would keep him alive. All the insecurities I had been harboring came rushing through. I had a responsibility that took precedence over everything else in my life. I was married to a man who had his own trouble, and he no longer was my first priority. I was so focused on this beautiful boy who needed all the love and attention. I tried to keep life altogether because my child deserved only the very best. Little by little things came crashing down all around us. My husband at the time could not handle his own trouble and the responsibility it took to raise a young child who was not that healthy. I was driving myself crazy trying to keep my family together, my baby alive and work all at the same time. I never knew how hard life could be, especially the way I chose it.

Growing up, I saw how my parents lived and tried to keep it all together. I saw their struggles with money and fighting with each other. It was an extremely stressful life. A life I did not realize how much it had molded me. I saw my own life unfold like theirs. I swore to myself I will always love my baby and not hurt him in any way. No matter what my struggles were, I would not put my troubles upon him.

Having a fear of where the money would come from and definitely not having enough to live on, the fear of not being able to provide for my child was staring me right in the face. I did not want my parents to come at me and say I told you so and take over my life. I did a lot of suffering in silence. I really had no one to turn too. I was alone with my baby, a husband who did not know what he wanted, and no support from anyone. When I think about it, I can't believe I got through that time in my life.

The worst was the fear of not being able to hide how much I did not know about life, how to handle money, being in a long-lasting relationship, raising a child in a loving environment and not fighting. However, what I learned most of all with all these fears, the more you resist it, the more it will persist.

Let's take money. I saw my parent's struggle the entire time I was in their lives. I saw them steal from Peter to Pay Paul to make ends meet. No matter how hard I saw them struggle with money, and try to get on track, there were always setbacks. There would be a bounced check that sent everything into a downward spiral, a child being hospitalized, needing medicine, a broken bone, a need for a bigger home, clothes, school supplies, etc…you get where I am going with this. On top of that, I found out when I was seventeen years old my parents were not biologically mine. All their money burdens were doubled because they took my sister and me in when we were young toddlers. I know. WHAT?

I always knew something was not right growing up. I felt it deep in my bones. I believe this is a significant reason why I have always felt the way I did growing up. My parents took my sister and I in as their own when we were toddlers. The family secret was revealed by someone who desperately wanted to hurt the family, not so much my sister and I. However, the worst landed on us, or I should say me. I took it very personally and everything I ever felt about growing up just made it worse. I took everything that ever happened, made it about me and knew I was treated how I deserved because I was never really theirs. It was the worst day of my life. I could have taken the treatment and the beatings, but knowing I was never their biological child made it so much worse. I knew I was punished for everyone else's actions and behavior.

Being a burden was huge in my life, a good forty-nine years. I always felt like I was someone who puts people in the poor house, and that is what I lived into. I created it all around me, even though it was not all mine to carry, I did it anyway. I could never be honest with the way I felt. Everyone would find out I was born to be a burden. I was sick up until I was forty-nine years old with asthma, eye problems, crazy spinal fluid build-up, allergies, sinus problems, joint problems…I mean really, look at what I bring to the table. That is what I lived into. However, I have realized everyone else has their own complete set of baggage. I carried the baggage for everyone.

I am the type of soul who takes on so many feelings and responsibilities, even the ones that are not mine to carry. I have always tried to lift the burden off of others and put them upon myself. So my fears ran very deep when it came to money, and everything else…it's the perfect way to keep me stuck.

We always want to give our children whatever we felt we did not get. We want them to have better opportunities, we don't want them to suffer or struggle as we did. We want them to have it all. Nevertheless, it never seems to work that way.

I have put myself in situations so I can give my son the best life he could possibly have. It all started when I was pregnant before marriage. I was twenty-three years old, just about two months out from having my baby. It was in November when we finally decided to get married so we could be a family our son would be happy in. The night of us saying "I do" by a judge, I knew I made a mistake. As much as I wanted my son to grow up in a home with a mother and a father, I knew we had too many problems to keep the marriage alive. Even knowing that we got married anyway.

It did not take long before the first bout of trouble. My son was about six months old. He was a sickly little baby, and we were on the cusp of our first break-up. It was one of the hardest things for me to go through. I was already estranged from the family I grew up in, and I had this little baby, hardly any money for myself. I was terrified, to say the least.

One thing I noticed was people were put right in front of me to utilize when I needed it the most. You know how they say blood is thicker than water. For me, the water was thicker than the blood. Somehow, in some way, I was able to get a credit card. I had a job that did not pay much. I had the most amazing woman take care of my baby, Aunt Mable. I found Aunt Mable through a lady I had worked with at the time. Angels were always in front of us. Aunt Mable helped me raise my son, get him off the bottle, potty train him and introduce him to soul food as well as soul music. It was a time where racism was at its peak, and we were the safest little white family participating in Maywood Park, Il. We were blessed in such a way, there are no words for my gratitude of Aunt Mable, she made sure my son was safe and was exposed to a fantastic culture.

Over time my soon to be ex-husband decided to come back home. We moved, tried to create a new life, but trouble continued to plague us. He worked so hard to be a husband and father while trying to overcome his own demons. Unfortunately, it got to the point of making the most significant decision to be unmarried for the sake of raising my son to be the best man he could be. It was rough, I was alone with my son, trying to do the right thing and give him the best life. However, he saw a lot that made an imprint. He had to leave his friends when we moved to live on our own, he was devastated. All I ever wanted was for him to have a great family, but he got a lot of fighting, a lot of dysfunction, and a lot of selling whatever I could to have money. It was not in my plan.

The fear he was going to grow up and do the same things his father did and be that kind of man terrified me. I put all my attention into him making sure that was not the same. I had him in counseling, Landmark Education,

I did whatever I could. I even allowed another man into our lives who I thought was going to be the perfect fit and give my child the experience he deserved.

As you are discovering, the fear of not being able to give my son a great life intertwines with the fear of making the right decision in a relationship. All we want is what's best for our children. We will sacrifice and maybe even suffer to give them the world. What we don't know, is that we lose ourselves in the process, we start to become fearful of what's ahead because we have seen what's behind. We don't want our children to deal with what we did, so we try to protect them from it. Even so, it comes anyway. Our children see through us and live it with us; they are never protected from it. They may have to go through it themselves, or maybe they have decided to go in another direction. It is never really our choice.

The fear plagues us in so many ways, we don't even realize it. I tried to protect my son from the lifestyle I had with his father. I did not want him to grow up with problems with alcohol or with the police. I wanted him to live a happy life without incident. I didn't want my child to be like me, I wanted him to be smarter than me, I wanted him to make better choices. However, he grew up just like his parents. He even has some of his step-father's traits.

Worry is the base of all fear. When we worry about what we don't want, we draw it to us faster than we realize. Everything I worried about the most for my son, he had to deal with anyway. I did not know at the time what I was actually saying, "Yes please I would like more of what I worry about the most."

All I can do in my present life is to keep talking about the lessons I have learned, and he has learned in a positive light. By doing so, he will start realizing it is okay not to be perfect and have problems. That we will get through it and everything will be okay. As long as we continue to see everything is actually happening for our highest good.

When I share my fears with my son, what I worried about when he got older, the more he realizes we all go through it. None of us will get through it unscathed. We must always learn and experience so we can grow. What I had always feared most of all was how my son would perceive me when he was older, if I were the perfect mom and did whatever it took, he would not find out I was learning as I was raising him. I did not want him to know I didn't have it all together. I was ashamed of myself because of all the choices I made for myself from emotions. However, I would never change a thing, because my son is everything to me and I want the world for him.

When I see him struggle, I see where my responsibility lies. I can't step in and help him. I can only pray he will listen and give himself a break. The fears we have for our children somehow, they will still have to face them. We really are not in control. The journey is the journey no matter what you believe in life. We all must learn and experience to grow to be our highest potential. When we discover this concept, we will be allowed to let our children go off and have their own learning lessons. We will then realize no matter how much we fear they will go through their own stuff, and there is nothing we can do about it.

What we truly fear is ourselves, not coming to terms with how extraordinary we genuinely are. It does not matter whether we went to college, have a high paying job or not. We are precisely who we are meant to be, and we need to quit fearing that.

From the relationships we have been in, we learn so much. When we keep going for the same type of partner, we are missing something in the teaching. Sometimes we need to go through a relationship over and over until we finally decide to love ourselves more. We may even pick one type of person then go with another kind, just to find out they are the same. When we can look at our self and realize why we attract that to us, we can change and move on.

I have had some pretty crappy relationships in my life, and they always seem to take a long time to break free from. What I have learned is I was afraid to be on my own. I was taught to find someone who had a great job and can take care of me. Well, I have found I am tired of waiting for that guy, and I need to take care of myself.

I am fifty years old, and I am finally on my own. I'm calling my own shots and doing my own thing. I'm also paying my own bills and loving every moment of it. I am learning what I like and don't like, who I want in my life and who I don't. When I meet my next partner, he will be my perfect match.

I no longer fear relationships. I have been through enough to know what is right for me and not. I have also been giving myself a lot of time to be with myself without trying to fill a void with men. Allowing myself to heal and love myself more than anyone else. That's right. I love myself more than anyone right now. Now I will let someone in my life who will love me as I would love me, and they will be loved more than they could have ever imaged.

I found when I accept the fear and move through it, I am creating the best life for myself.

Time Wasters

Have you ever realized how much time we actually waste in our lives when we are afraid to show people what we are really made of? Have you ever looked at the times where you would do anything else than what you know you need to do, even though you are very capable of doing it?

As I write, I realize how many times I have put off doing something, even though I knew I could do it. Have you ever experienced this yourself?

Why? Why do we do it? What is it that we are so afraid of? My take on my situation is, growing up it was never good enough. No matter what it was, I could have always done better. Even when I did my very best, it still was not good enough. So, for me, if I can't do the best of the best of the best, it is tough for me to get started. I have found I am an all or nothing type of gal. If I can't get it perfect, I am not going to do it at all. That is how I started learning how to waste time.

On the other hand, I had learned how to waste time because when I waited for the last minute, I would produce exceptional work that actually got an acknowledgment for it. So, I have learned last minute works. Even though last-minute puts massive stress on me, I always knew I would be doing my best work.

Isn't it funny how we start to learn and live into the untruths of our lives? Trying to live into someone else's expectations, and adopting that expectation as your own, is a rough life. I have done that my entire life, ever since I was young. I learned expectations are incredibly high, and if you don't meet them, trouble was your name.

Growing up I did not appreciate what my parents did for me. I was a child and did not know any better. However, as I had my own child and started working on myself through self-development along with tapping into my spiritual gifts, I realized I was raised in the perfect family.

It was not an easy family to grow up in. There was much struggle, and a lot of pent up anger turned toward the ones who could not really defend themselves. My Father was an angry man, someone who was extremely stressed out and did not know how to handle his anger. It was scary in the household. You did not know what would set him off or when all hell would break loose. My mother would take the brunt of the abuse. She would protect us as much as she could; until she couldn't do it anymore.

I really hate talking about this stuff. To better get out of your own way, you have to dig deep into your emotions to understand why, so you can shift and change. As I am sharing my story, I hope you are finding something about yourself you can relate to and change the way you're living your life. I know my parents did the best that they could with what they had. As a child, I did not understand that. I thought I was a bad kid who brought a lot of burden and heartache into their family.

I spoke earlier about always being sick, having severe asthma and being a burden, I would not wish on anyone. During my childhood I remember spending so much time in hospitals because I could never breathe; I was not like everyone else. I tried to help myself as much as possible, but it always got to a point where it went out of control. By the time that happened, I needed serious help. That meant a Doctor visit or a visit to the E.R. Anything would trigger an asthma attack, it did not matter, I never knew how bad the attack would be.

As an adult, diving into self-development, I did a lot of research about emotions and asthma. The more you are in situations that are emotional, violent, angry, desperate, it's hard to take in a deep breath which is life. It's like holding your breath waiting for the shoe to drop, anticipating your next beating.

I was born into a world where there was always struggle and not being able to breathe. When we are born, we adapt to the environment we are in and take on the energies of the home or homes we are in.

I am an Empath. Empaths are highly sensitive individuals, who have a keen ability to sense what people around them are thinking and feeling. Psychologists may use the term empath to describe a person that experiences a great deal of empathy, often to the point of taking on pain of others at their own expense. This is something that

I did my whole life. I did not realize I was an Empath until I was in my early thirties.

Asthma was a massive problem for me. I was always taking on other people's emotions and anxieties along with my own. Not being able to take in breath was not only my problem but the problems of the people closest to me. When I think about it, the family I was in was suffocating. Money was very tight. They were young themselves and had no idea what they were doing either. As an Empathic child, I took on all those burdens and responsibilities as my own. Therefore, I could not breathe in the physical sense. My awareness was so keen, breathing issues along with any other kind of illness I dealt with stemmed from emotions that were always around me. I also dealt with severe allergies which come from anger. I was a sick, angry little frustrated girl. I was not like everyone else, and in a house with so much violence in it, I took it all personal. I hated my body, my not being able to breathe, being allergic to everything, having to wear glasses and being different from everyone in my family. It seems to all make sense now.

You might be asking yourself right now, what does this have to do with wasting time? Great question. When not being able to do much because I was so sick, you get into the habit of either not doing things at all or waiting to the last minute. If a kid can get away with something, they will. If a kid has always been told they can't do something because they will get sick, the kid will start to believe the lie; otherwise, they will get sick.

This is how my habits started. I was always sick, so I bought into the lie and created patterns that left me feeling insecure and not worthy. I would try to find myself and figure out what it was I was good at or what I wanted to do. I was also trying to find someone who could take me away from the world I lived in so I could just be at peace. As I was trying to figure it out, I was not moving fast enough. The turmoil and anger were getting worse in our home. Nothing I did was done right or good enough. I was starting to really rebel from the family. All I wanted was to get out.

I found someone to get me out of my situation; that is how I got my son. I found the guy, got pregnant, got married thinking everything was going to be great, or at least better then what I already lived through. However, it did not take long for the insecurities I already dealt with kicked into high gear and I knew I was not ready for what was to come.

During this time, I learned if I were not inspired in my life, I would find anything to take me out of my reality. I learned how to create an escape, so I did not have to deal with my life.

One of my significant escapes is watching television. I would and sometimes still do get involved in a reality show, dramas, romance, even watch something I may not be interested in, but only to take me away from my own reality. I would also use wine as my escape as well. If I had something I needed to do, like clean the house or pay the bills, I would pour myself a glass of wine.

A glass of wine would lead to another, and another and another until I really didn't care. When my husband would come home, I would start a fight because I thought I was being judged. My time wasters were very debilitating. With my first husband, I was so busy trying to keep him out of jail, being faithful, driving him all over God's Country to get to work and back, it all came to a head. His last indiscretion threw me over the edge, and we divorced. I no longer wanted to keep the house clean, provide for him, I only did the bare minimum until I could get my son and me out.

The same thing with my second husband, I tried to be the best wife. I was so grateful for him, but it didn't take long for my efforts to go unnoticed. The more I was trying to be great and do it all, the more I went into a downward spiral, way out of control. Our finances went into the crapper, as I tried to hide the fact I had baggage and what I tried to create through business failed miserably. I was so ashamed and embarrassed to tell my husband I lost a lot of money. The creditors were calling, and I could no longer hide. This was the major event that kept my marriage in a downward spiral.

Not only did I never let myself off the hook for my financial mistakes, but my husband also didn't either. I spent many years torturing myself. There was not anything that I could have ever done to make up for the loss. I knew I would never be able to repay him. I would spend the rest of our lives trying to overcompensate for the mistake. There was nothing I could ever do that would help us to get back on track. My husband felt so betrayed and violated because I was not who he was expecting.

As the years went on, I became more and more disconnected. It did not matter what I did to bring in money, plan our anniversaries, a little weekend get-away here and there. I would try to create a business where we could be together more, all it did was create more resentment and disconnect between the two of us. I would dive into the T.V., into the wine and slowly be disconnected at home. I was sleeping in the basement. The house was a mess. The only time we got along is when we would talk on the phone. The distance seemed to work for us until it finally didn't.

When we become uninspired in our lives, we find escapes to go to so we can survive. Instead of me diving into something productive I was sabotaging myself. When I finally gave myself permission to make changes in my relationship; my entire world changed.

Now I live a life that is so different, all I have is my person to keep going along with my two little kitties. I found myself looking to participate in life instead of looking for an escape. I am inspired to live my life and do what I need to be healthy and happy.

Getting Trapped

One of the most significant ways in our lives of getting trapped is we believe the lies we tell ourselves. We have no way out, we are not the right person, we don't have the right body, we are not good enough, we can never make it on our own, and the worst "You made your bed now lay in it."

The expression, "I made my bed now I have to lay in it," is the worst lie we tell ourselves. We tend to punish ourselves in such a way, we will keep ourselves prisoner in our own lives. When we have children or responsibility, we will make sure we keep them first before ourselves. We start to believe our lives are over, we have nothing to look forward to, and we will never get our chance.

How many of you have felt that way or worse said it out loud? I know I have been guilty of it myself. However, you are only as stuck and miserable as you say you are. I have learned through working on myself, what you say about you is correct. If you say you can do it, YOU CAN. If you say you can't, YOU'RE RIGHT…YOU CAN'T!

Think about that for a second. What lies have you been telling yourself that you believe? What have your friends and family been saying to you that you think is true? What is your employer saying to you that you believe? Think about what you have been saying and listening to.

Did you know, when you say horrible things about your body, all your cells in your body are listening and giving you what you keep mentioning? It's incredible when you put emotional energy toward the comments you are making about yourself, you are then creating the world that you live in. When you feel victimized, it literally is from your own doing. Now do bad things happen to people? YES! The way we respond and react, we will make it much worse for ourselves.

How many times do you blame others for where you are in life? When we don't take responsibility for our own actions, we become weak in our lives. We start to create our own traps to keep us stuck where we are in life. We stop trying and we become complacent in our everyday life. We look for reasons why things don't work out, and we believe the excuses we are telling ourselves. We never take responsibility for what it is we are actually saying and doing.

I always become exhausted and cranky when I am not doing what I know I should be doing. While I am at work, I think about all the things I could be doing at home, and for my business, it's like I can't wait to get home. When I get back, I am exhausted, emotionally, physically tired and I don't do what I say I was going to do. By the time the weekend gets here, I will find myself watching T.V., sleeping and before I know its Monday. The more I continue this behavior, the harder it is to break free.

It takes a lot of positive talks to keep me on track. When I wake up in the morning, I say something positive about myself and my home. When I go to bed at night, I do the same thing over again. I make sure my brain wakes up happy and goes to sleep happy. Another thing I do every day is to make my bed. I never leave the house without making my bed. Even when I am late getting out the door, my bed is always made, and I am so grateful I have it to sleep in. I find the more grateful I am for everything in my life, the better I feel, and the more I stay on track. Now, don't think for a minute I don't have to work at this every day. I do. Some days are easier than others, but when I succeed, I feel so good. I just want to share my accomplishment with everyone who will listen.

Another way I will keep myself on track is to celebrate everything in my day. We tend to keep track of all the negativity, the mistakes that we perceive we've made. Every single one of us is on a journey. It's like taking classes in life. Some lessons we ace, and others we may struggle, while others we may perceive we failed. It's all perception, we are always learning and growing…the problem we don't celebrate ourselves. We need to know no matter what we can do anything we set our minds to and celebrate without worrying about other people's feelings.

When you wake up on time, and you have a smile on your face saying, "Good Morning," that is a significant accomplishment. You may deem it small, insignificant, or not even acknowledge it at all. You must remember, you just woke up happy, and you are sharing your smiling face. When you realize that, you will feel even better and start to make it a habit waking up happy.

Up until the time I have been in my own home, I would wake up so angry, I couldn't stand to be next to myself. My ex-husband could never understand how I felt that way or what I was talking about. He thought I was just mean and did not want to be around him. I was so trapped in my own story; I woke up miserable. Now living on my own, unmarried I wake up feeling fabulous. Even though I have things to do and responsibilities I am solely responsible for, I feel fantastic. In the last eight months, I have been on my own, I have woken up miserable only a few times. Either I was sick, or just a little from putting so many expectations on myself. That's it. I mostly feel amazing every day.

Here's another crazy trap we get ourselves in, expectation and setting the bar too high for ourselves. It is so hard to measure up to something we have no cap on. We all do it, especially the all or nothing group of people. We will tend to procrastinate and wait until the last minute to get something done. We beat ourselves up, thinking it could have been better when really it was perfect just the way it turned out. It is a terrible cycle we keep ourselves in.

Do you ever notice the amount of perfection we put on ourselves? It's perfection we will put on others as well. Growing up, we were expected to be a particular way, and when we did not measure up, it was not a good situation. I remember getting spanked for failing math in sixth grade. I had to stay in the house for two weeks doing math problems. I saw it as a punishment that fits a crime that taught me a huge lesson. Never let anyone see you struggle and don't let anyone know you don't know something. Always figure it out, or there will be hell to pay. There are so many little bits and pieces that pop in my head letting me know where some of my problems started. I don't want to blame my childhood, but it definitely begins in the environment I was brought up in.

However, that does not mean I don't take responsibility for my actions as an adult. Even a young adult I had to take responsibility for my actions. Too many of us blame everything on our parents and our upbringing. I have to admit; I was one of those people for some time. I was an angry little soul who felt abused and cheated.

The worst of it came on as I was going into my senior year of high school and found out my parents were my aunt and uncle. I was devastated when I realized my biological mother was who I called my aunt. I felt confused, betrayed, and hurt. I could not participate on any level. Everything that I had ever felt or gone through, I knew I was being punished, and I owed my parents more than I could ever pay back for taking me in their home. That was one of the worst times in my life.

As an adult, and participating in self-development, I realized I had the perfect childhood for my journey. I can help so many people from the experiences I had growing up, that it actually helped me be prepared for the life I chose. It's impressive as you grow older and mature how everything seems to be so different. I was given the gift to know how it felt when I was young, with my son I was able to understand him better and give him the space that he needed to grow.

I have also learned what not to do from my childhood. I never want to make anyone feel how I felt growing up. I am not always graceful in my communication, but I will always have someone's best interest in my heart and come from a place of love. One thing I am so proud of, I broke many cycles that plagued our family while raising my son. He is so respectful and loving toward everyone in his life. It is because I gave him space when he needed it. I helped him when he needed it. I never called him a name or made him feel bad about himself.

Most importantly I never blamed him for any of my problems. I always made sure he knew he was a blessing in my life and I am so grateful to be his mom. I am so proud of myself in this area of my life. It's the one thing I know, I did right.

There are things in my life. I am sharing with you, which by the way, I am kind of surprised because I did not think this book was going in this direction. I want you to realize no matter what happens in your life, you get to decide how you are going to be in life. Just because you have been through tough times, it does not mean you get to be a jerk in life. You always have an opportunity to be better than your circumstances and make a choice to be happy.

When you can make powerful choices for yourself, you can get out of the traps you have set for yourself. When you are inspired in your life and realize you can change your life, you can get out of your way. All you have to do is say yes and keep moving. What scares you the most is the direction you should be taking. Most of us hold ourselves prisoner when we are afraid. Just make that very first step, no matter how big or small and keep moving. You will see the trap you have set for you will start to dissipate.

Being Perfect

I have always tried to be the best version of myself. The problem is I have never allowed myself actually to be perfect. I have always found something wrong with me or anything it is that I am doing. This is something that plagues most of us throughout our life.

None of us really wake up in the morning and say "I want to be mediocre today." Usually, we wake up feeling like we have so much to do today and how will I achieve all of it. How can I fill my plate so full I can't possibly get it all done?

I am positive this sounds familiar to you because it is something I have always done and a lot of who I interact with is about the same way. I have listened to so many people tell me my story through their own account, it amazes me how we are all similar. I find comfort in knowing that I am not alone in the dysfunction.

We learn to be this way so we can get the approval of others, our family mostly, friends, co-workers, people who we may be romantically involved with. It's like we are striving for something we have been missing for so long. In the mean-time, we drive our selves crazy trying to achieve the almost impossible. We put ourselves in a position that actually causes harm to our confidence and security of who we are.

Isn't it amazing to realize how we torture, trap, and scrutinize ourselves in our life, so we can strive to be the best of the best? We tend to tear ourselves down and create a tremendous amount of worry and blame because we feel we can't measure up. We are chasing an accolade that never really comes, and it doesn't come because we will never allow it.

Answer me this...How many times do you acknowledge your accomplishments? How many times do you receive a compliment for the work you have done? How many times have you pointed out how you could have done something different or better for the outcome to be perfect? Think about these questions for a minute.

On average we do not acknowledge anything that we do. We take full advantage of ourselves. We never allow ourselves the satisfaction of doing a great job. We will pick at it and point out all the imperfections as we perceive it to be. It's no wonder why we doubt and feel miserable all the time. Why we think nothing is ever good enough, but the responsibility is on us. We are the ones who make our lives so difficult. We try to be better than our parents were, or people we are hanging around most. We are always in some crazy competition that we will never win, mostly because we will never allow ourselves to succeed.

Honestly, we are literally trying to be perfect in everything we do, we put the bar up so high for ourselves, we can't possibly reach it, far less actually touch it. We do this to ourselves and to other people. We will give someone a task to do, and guess what? We find everything wrong with it because it was not done the way we would have done it. Yet we didn't have the time ourselves to do it, and we still won't allow it to measure up.

  I was about twelve years old. It was the middle of winter. I was taught how to shovel the driveway properly. My first try at shoveling the driveway was not good enough. There was still snow on the driveway. It was not completely cleared off. For a twelve-year-old, it was pretty good. However, I had to go back outside and get everything off the driveway. I could not go back into the house until it was completely done. I was so angry; I remember yelling under my breath at my father when I was outside. I could not believe he was not out in the cold with me. The snow was so heavy; this was a time when we actually got real snow, not like the snow today. So, my twelve-year-old self took it to the extreme and made sure it was perfect. The end of the driveway, which by the way is the worst part to shovel, could not have anything on it. It all had to be shoveled off. At that point, I was so tired, but I did it anyway. I think my angry little person had so much rage I was able to use that energy to get the heavy snow and ice off.

  Now in my life, the driveway for me is an OCD thing. The snow piles have to be perfect, and the driveway has to look as if the snow was never there. I have done this my whole adult life. I will shovel a particular way, to get every bit off, and honestly, I don't want anyone's help, because it won't be done the way I need it done. It makes me crazy when I see other people with their driveways, and they do it just good enough to get their car in or out. I am telling you it makes me crazy. I have to try not to notice other people's driveway literally, so I don't make people wrong inside of my head.

When the driveway was complete, and I got to go back in, I was so proud of myself. I would be chewing at the bit waiting for my father to say what a great job I did. He would look at it to make sure there was no snow, and that was it. Not "Great Job," no "WOW I can't believe you got the end of the driveway" ...NOTHING. In my head, it was not good enough, so I always did whatever it took just to get a good job from him. I think that is why I still to this day, shovel the driveway the way I do. Instead of waiting for someone to say, "Great Job," I tell myself GREAT JOB, YOU ARE AMAZING.

It was the same thing when we had to clean the house. We had our chores, and we had to go through the white glove test. If it was not done to my parents' satisfaction, we had to do it all over. I hated cleaning. I hated spending hours and hours trying to make something clean enough. If we had company coming, there would be all kinds of yelling, screaming and fighting because we were not doing it right or fast enough. It was horrible. I hated the holidays because nothing was ever good enough. What's crazy, I have done the same thing most of my adult life. Finally living on my own, I allowed myself to calm down and keep everything the way I like it. I will still sometimes yell at the Kitties because they are messing up what I am creating, but I realize how much I love my space the way it is. It's a process that is slowly changing and how I get it done is perfect. I am no longer stressing about making it perfect.

Think about it, when you are hosting a party, and the cleaning is finally all done, the guests arrive, are you receiving the compliments or are you pointing out what you could have done better? Maybe you are pointing out how the napkins don't really match the table. I challenge you to do whatever it is you have planned, let it be, don't make it perfect. Allow something to be undone. The challenge is to receive the compliment and say, "THANK YOU." That's all. Nothing else, don't elaborate. Just say "THANK YOU." You will find everything was perfect, even when you left something undone. I know, it's hard, trust me, you won't regret it. You will start to feel the confidence in yourself with a job well done.

This is something we have learned long ago, it's not our parents' fault…it's what they have learned from their parents, and right down the line. It's generations of building on one another, and we take it to the extreme. There is no blame to place, it's just to acknowledge and realize that however, we do something, it's perfect just the way it is.

About a month ago, I was doing some Angel Writing, communicating with my Angels and they shared with me the name of this book I am writing. They told me I needed just to sit down and start writing and it will all start to unfold. I wrote the title and let it sit. Every time I pulled out my journal to write, the book kept coming up. They told me to start writing no matter where you're at, work, at home, it did not matter, just write, just do it.

For whatever reason, we get into our heads about how things should be, because that is how someone, somewhere did it. We never really take into consideration that it can be done another way. There is no real right or wrong way to do something, just as long as we do it. Over time we start to see what we can do differently to make a stronger impact or maybe learn something new along the way. Most importantly we begin to see how powerful we truly are instead of playing small in our lives.

It's funny, we never consider ourselves an expert unless someone who we respect says we are. We are always looking for approval before we allow ourselves to really do something big, or even small, whatever it is that we are doing. It holds us back in our everyday life. It's time we really start learning to go within and trust that we are an expert in whatever it is that we are doing, and just do it. We get so trapped in what we think other people would say, so we won't try, or we wait until the last minute.

Start to look at what you want to achieve in your life and don't worry about anyone else. Give yourself permission to live your life powerfully.

Our Perception

At this point, I think you are starting to realize how all these different topics we have been talking about really wreak havoc on our perception of ourselves and what people think of us. We are so afraid of making a mistake; we will keep ourselves stuck no matter how unhappy or sad we are.

When we are young, we make lots of decisions about how we will not put ourselves in certain situations depending on how the people around us react. I coached a young man in his thirties a few years back. He had such a hard time making his own big decisions. He would stay in a career where he was comfortable just because he needed the approval of others to make a move. He wanted to branch out into music, but not enough people said, "Yes, that's a great idea," what he listened to was the people who said; "You're too old." He continued to long for his dreams but would not go out and grasp them. I asked him, "When was the first time you made a decision for yourself, and you got a response that made you feel bad about it"? He said when he was in kindergarten, he got his own clothes, picked out his socks that he loved and when he got to school the kids laughed at him. He said," he cried and felt bad." He never picked out his own clothes and socks after that, his mom did it. I shared with him; his little kindergarten self has been driving his life. He would not make any big decisions for himself because he was afraid of what people would say or do. He decided in that moment of being made fun of, he could not be trusted to make his own decisions. Now he waits for massive approval before he makes his move. He thought about what I shared with him, later that day, he said to me, "Thank you, and thank you for letting me see a different perspective in my behavior."

The little five-year-old perception decided if I choose my own clothes and socks, I will be made fun of and feel stupid. I am never doing that again… he then started to live in that perception and decision. We all do it, we make these decisions all the time, and we are not even aware of it.

My body has always been a focal point for men, and I have always hated it. I never really realized my body until I was in sixth grade. I was eleven years old; a lot was going on in my life. We were switching schools; we went from a private school to a public school. I was terrified of the kids. The first day of school I did not feel good, I couldn't breathe. I went to school and had to bring my medicine to the nurse's office. I knew it was going to be a rough day. We were not allowed to keep our medicine on our person. As the morning went on my breathing got worse and worse, I kept asking to go to the nurse so I can use my inhaler. I was a sweaty mess, I struggled so hard to breathe my hair was dripping wet. The nurse would not let me take another puff of my inhaler, she said: "I have taken enough." She ended up calling my parents to pick me up and take me to the doctor. By the time my father came, I was drenched in sweat. My arms were like unbendable sticks to keep my head down and chest open. I could barely move. Getting to the doctor felt like forever. I had to wait for my father to leave work to come and get me from school so we could make our way to the doctor's office. I hated going to his office, the drive was so long, and when I couldn't breathe it was the worst. We were driving down North Avenue in the middle of the day, and it was all stop and go. I remember sweat dripping down my face. I really thought I was going to suffocate. The more I could not breathe the more frightened I became. When we finally arrived at the office, the doctor gave me a shot to open my lungs and give me an IV drip to get medicine in my system. I was still not breathing, and my father was instructed to take me to the hospital. As soon as I heard hospital, I got sick all over his office in front of other kids who were there. I was so embarrassed and scared.

    I hated the hospital, it was a constant sticking of needles, and I felt all alone, even though my mother was always with me, I felt lonely and scared. I was in there for a week. I had to take a high dose of steroids, and new medicine. The worst part, I was told I could no longer eat ice-cream, chocolate, and eggs. For a young person who had already loved that food, it was hard to be told I could not have it anymore. It was more of what was being taken from me along with being different from everyone else.

    As time went on the steroids were wreaking havoc on my body, I developed early and started going through puberty in the sixth grade. I got my period during swimming class for the first time, it was awful. My breasts were huge, and the boys loved it, I didn't know why, but they did. I hated my body so much, I did not understand why this was happening to me, it was a terrible time. My whole body changed on the steroids, along with my attitude and behavior. At that time, we had no idea the effects steroids had on a person for long stints of time. When the doctor realized I had been on the steroids for a year, he immediately took me off. There was no weaning me off, it was cold turkey. As an adult now, I know that was not a good idea, but back then no one really knew how bad steroids were for people, and you had to be weaned off slowly for your body to adjust. I did not get that luxury and my body suffered for it.

In Jr. High, a student in my English class took it upon himself to grab my breast as he was taking his seat. He squeezed it so hard, the pain was unbearable; just so he could feel if it was real. It was one of the most painful moments I had ever encountered. I did not understand what was happening. I knew I was violated, and my god did it hurt. The overuse of steroids amplified the pain my body felt. I could not understand why I had to feel so much pain all the time, my breasts were always so sensitive, especially around my period. I could barely touch them myself. When I was a freshman in high school, the neighborhood store down the street from where we lived, the owner took it upon himself to lure me into the back room on Sunday night. He wanted to show me what boys liked and started to touch my breasts. I did not know what to do, I had known this man most of our life. He owned the little store. Thank goodness someone came into the store. As I heard the doorbell ring as someone walked in, I made my escape and ran home. I was terrified, I had no idea what to do. Should I tell my parents? Would they believe me? I was afraid of getting into trouble. I really thought I did something wrong. I never went back into that store again.

My perception of my body was that I was dirty and disgusting because boys and old men would not leave my chest alone. I did not like it, and I tried to hide as much as possible. The more I tried to hide my chest the more attention I seemed to get.

After that event in high school, I tried to protect myself, so I did not have to deal with unwanted groping. Thus, the unwanted, yet wanted weight started to pile on my body. Even to this day, I have trouble with my body weight. My body is like a yoyo, when I am secure with myself, the weight I carry falls off. As soon as I feel the need for protection of any kind the weight piles on. I am noticing, whatever it is that I am experiencing will dictate how my weight will go.

The more I work on myself and deal with the emotions from my past, the more secure I am with me. Living alone has shown me how much I have let go from past pain. I have learned that it is okay to be seen and to participate with people. I am not giving myself up but loving life and enjoying my true self. The first six months of living by myself, I loved it so much I did not want anyone to come in and take it or convince me to be with them. So, I allowed the weight to pile on. It was my defense mechanism to keep unwanted attention away from me so I can continue to heal.

We make decisions in our life based on our perception of the experiences we are having in life. When we are young, we don't understand, and we decide from that point of view how we will stay safe. It does not matter how old we get, those little people inside of us keep us safe from what we perceive as harmful to our person.

The five-year-old who wore crazy socks to school, in his thirties still did not make decisions based on his experience. For me, my weight is my defense in case someone tries to take away from me what I am creating.

Now is the time to realize how are you being in life? Who is actually running your life? Are YOU or YOUR younger self running your life? It's a lot to think about, trust me. I have been putting in the work. Now being un-married for the second time, I love living on my own. However, I have created protection around me to keep me safe. Right now, as I am writing, I realize how I am keeping myself free from men. The work I continue to do on myself is mind-blowing. When you dive into what is going on around you, writing your emotions down, along with how things are occurring for you, you begin to get a handle on what is actually happening to you, only then you can make changes for your life that work for you.

Our perceptions are based on one side. Our side. We see things happening as if it is only us in the story. Realistically, there are many involved in the story, but we only get our perception, and we then base our life on just that, our own self. When I am with clients, I ask them to look at the bigger perspective of what is happening. When you do, you start to see the bigger picture. Maybe you are a character in a bigger picture, and honestly, it may not be just about you.

As I just wrote about the bigger picture, in my mind's eyes, I saw I was the last young girl the store owner assaulted. I was just a character in the bigger picture of him finally getting caught and losing everything. He will never have another opportunity to prey on a young girl again.

I realize that not all men who resemble my offender are bad men. However, I have always seen them that way. A particular look of a man has still triggered the memory of the offense. Even now, I am at the age of my offender, and I have to start looking at men differently. I have to quit protecting myself against them because now they are my peers. This is a real reason why I keep myself fluffy.

Even the way we react or respond is all based on our perception. We won't really hear or try to understand a situation, because our wounded little selves will take us back to a time where we felt not heard or bad about ourselves. We decided a long time ago if a situation does not seem right for us, to do whatever it takes to protect our person. Our little self has gone into protective mode and automatically reacts accordingly to get us out of any situation we perceive as harmful. However, when we start to get an understanding of the whole experience, we would then begin to respond differently and not feel threatened. We would be coming from a place where we start to understand what was happening and see the situation differently. When we are away from the situation for a few minutes or even a day, we will come back and actually see what occurred. This is when we start to learn how to see the bigger picture and start viewing things differently.

In my process of understanding and healing, I have to be able to look at a particular aging man and not see the Little Store Owner. I need to start looking at the face before me without judgment.

The EGO

Another way that keeps us stuck and not moving forward in our lives is our EGO. It is our inner self that we have created agreements with to keep us safe. The Ego is our inner child, young person, and young adult. Wherever we needed protection, we made an agreement with our ego self to keep us safe.

The other part of the ego is our inability to see our responsibility, or we act as if we are the only person that matters. We are not able to apologize, and we always blame others for our lives.

I have operated from both sides of my ego through the years. As I have been learning about myself and why I do the things that I do or don't do, I have come to learn from the ego who protects me and the ego who does not want to be responsible.

Every single thing that goes on in our life, we have some sort of responsibility in. Now, I can feel you getting defensive and saying, "You don't know what I have been through." In that, you are right. I don't. However, what I do know is that, no matter what has happened, taking responsibility makes a difference.

I grew up in an angry household. It was not like that all the time. However, when times were tight, it was the worst. As a child who absorbs the energies of other people around me, I became an angry child who wanted everyone to hurt who hurt me. As I got older and started working on myself, I was able to let go of the debilitating anger that kept me held prisoner.

I had to realize that as an Empath I absorbed the energy and emotions around me, they were not always my emotions. I remember being happy, but when things were bad at home, I remember being angry to the point I would have a rage that came from my toes all the way up. I would clench my fists, and I would throw my glasses or hit myself, I needed that outlet to release the rage. I had no idea what was happening to me then. As an adult and learning about my spiritual gifts, I now understand and take responsibility for my actions.

I was so angry and full of resentment because I was not seeing the bigger picture. I felt sorry for myself, and I reacted like a victim. When I was told my parents were not my biological parents, and my aunt was my biological mother. I felt so betrayed and started to go down a path of anger. I felt as though the world owed me something. I would get even angrier when I realized how much of the physical abuse and mental abuse I dealt with. I could not understand my childhood at all. I was a complete mess. I could not wait to get away from my parents' house and everyone in it.

I would date guys who were not good for me and treated me the way my father did. At the time I did not see it that way. However, in hindsight that is what I was doing. I did not take responsibility for my own feelings and what happened, so I turned myself into a victim. My first husband was the perfect person to get me out of my situation. My second husband was supposed to be the right guy to marry so everyone would be proud of me. I was not taking responsibility for my own person. However, in saying that, I would not change anything about my life, because who I am today is because of all of it. I also received the greatest gift of my life from my first husband…my son.

The ego is very tricky if you are not paying attention or even aware. Many of us put ourselves into situations we know are not ultimately good for us, but we do it for many reasons. It could be that we need to get rescued, prove something to someone, or prove something to our own selves. Why we do it is endless, and it's unique to each of our situations. A lot of women will stay in a bad relationship to make sure their children are taken care of; not realizing their good intentions can hurt the children and keep the cycles going.

I have shared that my life was not so easy growing up. It was difficult for all in the family. As an adult, I can understand some of it, but as a child, I didn't get any of it. I was a hurt angry little girl. My perception of my father was a very angry mean person.

Along with being very violent, he directed his behavior in a very toxic and debilitating manner to us. There was constant fighting in the house. It didn't matter what was happening, someone was experiencing his wrath.
My father was violent toward our mother. As a child, it was so hard to know what was happening and we

could not do anything about it. All we could do was scream, cry and hope he did not come after us. I am not sharing this to be mean, just to illustrate how as children our egos step in and start to protect us from situations that are not good so we can survive. Our mother took a lot of the abuse physically, mentally and emotionally. I watched her take whatever came to her. There were times where I just wanted to jump in and protect her, but I was just a kid. When I got a little older and a little confident, I started to exercise my voice and stand up to him. Sometimes it worked. Most times it did not, but I never gave up.

When I was young, I remember three different occasions on a Friday night my father packed his clothes into black plastic bags, sat in the dining room at the table crying and saying he was sorry. He made sure he said goodbye to each of us while my mother was on the couch. I was screaming inside of myself saying "Just GO!" The night ticked away, we had to go to bed and he was still at the dining room table. When we awoke on Saturday morning, he was still there, and no one said a word. I was devastated and angry that my mother didn't kick him out. He got to be there yet again to make our lives miserable. As a child, I did not understand her fears of raising us on her own. As an adult I do. I held a lot of resentment toward my mother. I didn't think she protected us enough. However, she defended us the best way she knew how. I always thought, even as a child, we would have done so much better without him. At least we would all be happy, or really, I would have been satisfied.

When you start to see the bigger picture, you can see how you are operating in your life, as a victim, an abuser yourself, or someone who is taking charge and making things happen positively. It takes time to figure it all out if you are willing to be responsible and start taking care of yourself by doing some self-development.

I once had someone say to me, why do you keep doing these classes that make you emotional and drudge up stuff from the past? I don't get it. Why not just leave it alone? I said to her because I don't want to continue to live my life like this. I want to be happy and free from the chains of my life. I don't want to keep blaming my life on my past. When you get the big picture, you see there was something for you to learn in all of it. She didn't understand, and we just left it alone. However, I continue to educate myself and see different perspectives so I can powerfully rewrite my past.

One of the benefits of finally letting go of your past is healing. Once you heal and let it go, your ego no longer has to step in and take over. You will be able to start living your life powerfully.

Think about what was it that stopped you in your life? What was it that had you react badly? What had you step back and not participate? These are all great trigger questions that will allow you to see the bigger picture of what you went through.

Once you start to understand there is always something for us to learn and teach; we can understand why we went through what we did. We can understand

why we kept ourselves from participating or maybe speaking up. We can better understand why we react to certain words or sounds. We can understand why we respond to particular gestures or pats on the head or even an arm grab. When we can really look at it from different angles, we no longer will allow ourselves to be affected in that way; that's where the healing begins.

Re-Writing My Past

One of the biggest things I have learned over the years is to identify my ego, decide who is running it and for what reason, also to allow myself to see a different perspective, and start rewriting my past.

Rewrite my past? Yes, you may not be able to change the events that occurred in your past. You can undoubtedly rewrite your perspective and change how you respond to your past. It is a technique that will help you get out of your own way and start to live your life powerfully.

When you can see different perspectives, other than the one from the event, you can start to see your parts and understand others along with taking your responsibility.

As I have shared, I found out my parents were not biologically mine, and I was devastated. I turned into an angry person who just wanted everyone around me to be in just as much pain as I was. I felt like I was a burden, I was unlovable, and I did not really belong to anyone. I lived in this anger for many years. It got worse when I had my own child. I loved him so much; I could not imagine not being with him or loving him as much as I did. I could never imagine hurting him the way I was hurt.

It was toward the end of my first marriage that I started to do the self-development. I worked for a church that had an interim pastor who was hip on spirituality and self-improvement. She was a wonderful mentor for me. Pastor Mary helped me see things are more significant than we know them to be. She taught me there was more to a story then what was right in front of me. She gave me my first three books to read, The Four Agreements, Secrets of The Vine, and the Prayer of Jabez to get me started on my journey.

Pastor Mary is a woman who sees beyond what was in front of her. She taught me how to look at the bigger picture of a situation and tune into my own spiritual self. Pastor Mary taught me I was an extraordinary person who has a lot of love to share. She also taught me I was a unique person, and there was nothing wrong with me. Pastor Mary also showed me God loves me. He could never be disappointed in me. With that, I should never be cruel or punish myself any longer. Even writing that last sentence was kind of hard. I still can be cruel to myself, and punish myself in ways that will keep me held back in life. It is definitely something I continue to practice.

As I began to deal with my deep-rooted anger with my parents and my family, I realized I was raised in the perfect environment. I want to make sure it's clear. It took a lot of work on my part to be able to even say this. Now, I have learned to trust and love again. I learned to laugh and have fun. I learned there are always reasons why things happen the way they do. I am not saying what I have been through was right, what I am saying is, when I look back at all of it, I can help so many people because of it. I understand that because of the experiences I went through I can relate to many people. They trust me and share their story so I can help them see something different for themselves. They learn to let go of what pains them and live a beautiful life.

I realize I had to be raised by my aunt and uncle. I learned many lessons because I have a lot to do and teach. I needed to be able to rewrite my own story so I could show someone else to do the same so they can let go and live. I also realize the events that have occurred in my life brought Angels to me, so I can continue to be guided and keep moving forward in my life. When we don't realize things are actually happening for our highest good, we miss out. We miss out on the signs and the angels who are being put in front of us to be guided through the darkness into the light. When we can move forward, we can assure someone else that their life will be okay.

I also realize my parents, who raised me, sacrificed quite a bit in their lives. It could not have been easy raising someone else's children in addition to their own child. They went from a three-person family to a five-person family, two of which were not their own. Even though I did not have a picture-perfect life, it was perfect for me. I have gained more knowledge and compassion than I ever imagined.

I have rewritten my life, and I am living it powerfully. I have chosen not to be a victim because a victim tends to be helpless and I am someone who will overcome anything.

When I look at my son and the way I have raised him, I am genuinely proud of myself. I knew how I wanted him to be in life, and that is how I raised him. It did not matter what we went through, I wanted him always to love and be kind to people. I see my son giving love to everyone around him. He is kind and very strong willed as well. I could not be any prouder of him. The way he handles life and loves the people around him, I know that by rewriting my past I gave him a totally different experience from what I had.

The other thing that is amazing about rewriting your past is the fact you no longer stay stuck in being angry. No matter what happens in your life, you treat others with the utmost love and respect, even those who do not treat you the same.

I was able to reconnect with my sister for a short time by rewriting my past and being compassionate toward her. We had never really gotten along. In fact, we actually have always hated each other. I know it is a strong word, but it's true. We grew up in an angry, violent household, so there were a lot of emotions and words felt and said by all. How I felt about my sister was not kind, but that is how it was.

We reconnected for a couple of years. My sister was on the outs from our family, and she really needed someone. She reached out to me, I opened my heart. We talked a lot and decided to be sisters. For a good year or so we talked for hours almost every day. I really thought that we were on the mend. We discussed our lives, our biological family, trying to piece it all together. Then something happened. I am not sure what exactly, I have a feeling she was being accepted back into our family. She loves them so much. It crushed her to be on the outs. When she saw her opportunity to get back in, she took it to be in good graces again. I am not going to tell you I wasn't hurt by it, because I was. However, I knew she could not live without them. I had over twenty-six years of practice.

The conversations with my sister dwindled down to nothing until there were no more. The last time I spoke to her was when I was becoming unmarried, and she wanted to know where I got my new last name. I told her it was from my biological Father's middle name. She said, it makes sense, and that was it. Never to be heard from again. It has been a year now. I am happy, and I know she is too. I was able to give her the love she needed and help her to release the negative emotions that were keeping her stuck. That was my place in her life at that time. If we ever speak again, I will invite her back in.

These are the gifts you receive when you start to see life more significant than yourself. I realize that no matter what happens I am here for a purpose, and that purpose is to help others through all of my life experiences. If I always saw the world attacking me and keeping me down, I could not help anyone. I would not be able to use my spiritual gifts, because I would not have even known I possessed such beautiful gifts.

No matter what we have been through in life, we have to be able to see the bigger perspective. My best friend Mary lost her daughter tragically; Someone decided she was no longer going to live on this earth, so he took her life. Mary went through a time in her life, and she still continues to, where every mother's worst fear comes true. Mary has had to endure such grief on top of dealing with the legality around her daughter's death. It truly is every parent's worst nightmare. However, Mary continues to handle herself with such grace and ease. She talks about her daughter every day and keeps her spirit alive. This is one of the most painful things Mary has ever dealt with, how Mary is in life is remarkable. You would never know her situation unless she actually had a conversation with you about it. My friend does not treat people horribly, Mary gets up every day no matter how difficult and keeps moving forward. She knows there is more to life than what is in front of her and her pain.

When you are rewriting your past and really looking at the bigger picture, you can really make a difference in life. I think that is why we are all here. How can we experience what goes on during our time here on earth and still make a significant difference? Some people have gone through worse things, live powerfully and make a difference. There are others whose whole life crumbles down, and people just feel sorry for themselves. Ask yourself, "Where do I want to be in my life?" Do you want people to admire you or feel sorry for you? We always have that choice.

It's been six years since Mary's daughter was taken from us and it feels like it just happened. What is impressive to me about her, the grace and ease you see in her everyday living. I said it before; you would have never guessed what has been going on in her life unless she actually told you. Every day her heart breaks thinking about her daughter and yet she teaches people to be kind to one another no matter what. This woman is such an inspiration to me, and I love the fact our energy matches, and we are the best of friends.

This is something so essential to grasp. No matter what has gone on in our lives, we owe it to ourselves to be kind, loving and forgiving. Being kind, loving and forgiving only really begin after we rewrite our past.

Forgiving

Forgiving. What does that word mean, why do we have to forgive, and who do we have to forgive?

Forgiveness is an action that we have such a hard time doing. As humans, we want to be right and stand in our own convictions. However, that is not always for our highest good and the highest good of others.

When we hold onto pain, and we don't forgive we actually stay a prisoner in our own life. It is hard for us to love, trust and move on. We become so angry and bitter we can't see past our own self.

I was an angry person. I can't stress to you the magnitude of my anger. I felt so betrayed by the people closes to me called my family, I could not trust myself or anyone else. I didn't love myself, which means I turned into a mean girl for some time. I walked around as the world owed me something and I was the most important person. I would only see what I wanted. It did not matter to me what others needed.

When I became pregnant, I had a chip on my shoulder that was seen by all except for me. I had a tone in my voice that was deep down angry and hurt. I chose a life that would make sure I suffered as I thought that's what I deserved. There is an old saying "Make your bed and lie in it." That was the theme of my first marriage. I did not have anyone to turn to when times were tough, and yet I had Angels placed all around me when I was at the end of my rope.

When I gave birth to my son, I had so much overwhelming love for him. I could not imagine not being there for him or helping him in any way. I swore no matter what happened in my life, my child will be number one, as well as, it did not matter what he would ever do, I will never abandon him. My son is my most magnificent Angel. He has taught me so much about love, and he still continues to teach me.

I had such a hard time letting go of the betrayal and the abuse. I hate saying abuse, but there is no other way to say it. It took me so many years to let go. I had been a tortured soul for such a long time until I had my Angels placed right in front of me. I was taught forgiveness was not about saying what took place was okay, it was about saying I will no longer be a prisoner to the experience and the person. When I forgave the experience, I stopped holding myself prisoner making myself wrong, and finally let go.

The best thing I have found is when you don't forgive the offender, that person who was a part of the experience, you will have a terrible time making heads or tails of why it happened. It took a long time for me to understand that concept. I didn't realize you can forgive the person and yourself, and not allow the person back into your life. I found it was okay to leave the relationship as it was and not have to participate again. When I understood these things about forgiveness, I literally set myself free. Now, it does not mean that all of a sudden you stop suffering. It truly does take a process, but it can go as slow or as fast as you want. For me, it took a while until I finally decided not to make myself suffer any longer.

Always remember, when you forgive someone, you are setting them free. My past no longer has power over me. When you forgive, you also do not have to invite participants back into your life. It just means you are no longer a prisoner to whatever happened. You learn and grow from it.

The biggest problem I had was forgiving me. Forgiving yourself, I found, was one of the hardest things I ever had to do. I had to take responsibility for my actions and love myself enough to let it go.

I blamed myself for everything that happened. I hated who I was, the burden, the problem, the unlovable, the trouble maker, the dependent. The list can go on and on. That is how I felt. Like I said earlier, I did not realize that I was an Empath, so I took on all my emotional baggage including everyone else around me. For a long time, I really felt sorry for myself. I had that victim mentality until I realized it did not serve me. It took a lot of practice to look in the mirror and just love me for me, without everyone else's baggage including my own.

I had to realize that we are all the same trying to figure it all out, and if I can forgive another, I should be able to let myself off the hook as well.

Now to put this all into perspective, I am fifty years old, I finally love me, trust me, set myself free and I am living on my own terms. I practice every day letting go. I Angel Write and communicate with my Angels every day. I see the bigger picture and why everything worked out the way that it did. I can't imagine my life any other way in present time.

Forgiveness is one of the most important things we need to practice daily. As we breathe air, we need to forgive. I bet you don't even realize how much stuff that is in your own life you are punishing yourself for…maybe a job lost, a relationship gone wrong, money problems, a bad decision, words said. We find so many ways to punish ourselves; we don't even realize that it is happening.

We start to realize it when we get older and all of a sudden everything bubbles up in our lives. You may begin to feel sad, depressed, may have a little anxiety, maybe there is something in someone you just can't stand. There are all kinds of clever ways we punish who we are. We need to have the courage to stand tall and take responsibility for who we are and make the change.

One of the reasons it is so hard to forgive ourselves is being without our drama; we don't know how to be in life. We start to panic and freak out when what we have always known is finally gone. We begin to look for ways to fill the void so we can feel somewhat normal. We have been living a particular way our whole life. It is really all we know. When it's finally gone, we don't know what to do with ourselves.

Think about it. What did you feel after a break-up, a job loss, the end of a friendship or after someone close to you passes away? We are overwhelmed with the pain we are trying desperately to replace. That is why so many people hang on to their baggage. They don't know how to be with the emptiness, the quietness, the calmness, the peacefulness…they start to look for more things to fill the void.

It's the perfect opportunity to be with the emptiness and learn from it, so we can grow healthy and fill the void with love and compassion and forgiveness. Forgiveness always sets us free.

Who Am I?

When we forgive and finally let go of what holds us back, we have an empty feeling inside us that needs to be nurtured and loved. We start to wonder "who am I without the drama." We begin to focus on this void inside of us and what we should do to fill it.

Letting go of the old way of being, that person we have been holding on so tight for so long. We are afraid to let go of what makes us walk into the unknown of who we are. Sometimes we would rather stay stuck because it's what we know and that is what is comfortable for us. It seems better than the unknowing, being uncomfortable and not being in control that we are embarking on.

It's the old saying, "you can take the girl out of the city, but you can't take the city out of the girl." We hold on so tight to what we know. When we are so tired of the drama, and we have no other choice then to let go, that's when you allow the emptiness to come in.

After fifty years and living on my own for the very first time. I don't have anyone to look after other than my kitties. It is me and me alone. I finally decided to end the relationship that was not going anywhere but constant Fight Ville. I could not take it anymore. We both deserved so much more in life than what we were living.

I had no idea where I was going to live. I had no idea what I wanted. How was I going to furnish my place? Was I going just to move in and see what happened or was

I going to make it my home? I had no idea what I really liked or didn't like. My friends kept giving me things so I would have what I needed. I was grateful, but I had no idea what I was going to do with it.

When I found my new home, moved in, everything went into its perfect place. It amazed me how everything matched when it came from multiple people. It was as if I finally met up with my true self and now, we get to continue on our journey. What a fantastic feeling to have everything just fall right into place so quickly. It does not matter how small my home is, or where it's at, my new home is where I belong.

The one thing that surprised me about my home, I never felt like something was missing. I felt like I am right where I need to be. I started to realize I really don't have anything to fight about, complain about, or even be unhappy. I truly love every bit of my new home; I say it every day getting up from bed, and coming home from work, right as I am going to bed. I have never felt so comfortable and safe my entire life. For the first time in my whole life I am truly home. I am forever grateful.

My home allows me to be at peace and really discover who I am. I decide what I want in my life and what I don't want. These past nine months have been amazing. The fight that has always been in me has disappeared. I genuinely do not have to fight to defend myself anymore. The peace is well overdue and quite welcomed to my life.

I am also becoming very patient in my life. I find I am not losing my temper and getting crazy over the small stuff or even the big things. I know deep down, I am right where I need to be, and I know everything is working out for my highest good.

I wake up in the morning feeling refreshed and filled with gratitude. I keep my home clean and organized because I am inspired to live the life I have always desired. It's like a miracle has happened in my life. I surprise myself every day by who I am, my true Rita.

I have never been able to be my true self. I have always been trying to be the person everyone else wants me to be, and it's never good enough. I have taken classes, gotten great jobs, done great things, but nothing has ever gotten me to who I truly am. Being in my own home, expressing my true self, allows me to appreciate my expression in which I am. I have never felt more confident in who I am as I do today.

Letting go and finding my true self has led to great opportunities for myself. My spiritual gifts have come in so strong; I can help more people than ever. I am getting ready to do a class for two hundred people in Angel Writing. It has been fantastic learning, growing and not being afraid to express my true self. I love it.

This is what I hope for each and every one of you who is reading my book. When you are forgiving, letting go, and finally discovering who you really are, so many wonderful opportunities open up like magic. When you are free from the anger, you can receive the opportunities coming to you. You will know when to say yes, and when to say no, and you won't feel guilty saying no.

Saying NO

Have you ever had a hard time saying no…? Most of us do. We are always saying yes and filling our plates as full as possible. This is another way we keep ourselves stuck.

We just keep saying yes to everything. We believe if we help as many people as we can, we will feel so much better about ourselves. That's not true. We actually feel bombarded and aggravated at ourselves, but there is still a part of us that feels grateful that people can't live without us. We get this weird confirmation that we are important; meanwhile, we are being taken advantage of, and our energy is being drained.

You know the people I am talking about…A 'Yes' Person. I am sure you have dabbled yourself. For me, I would say yes to everything and volunteer my husband to participate. I was the do it all girl, no matter what was going on I would find a way. I would also, complain that I said yes, I would have anxiety up until the time I was supposed to do what I said I would do. I would drive myself crazy along with my family.

When I would say yes to everything, I did not feel good about myself at all. I felt like the more I did for people, the less likely they would find out what a fraud I was. However, there is always something we get out of that behavior. Amid all the praising, it's the perfect place to hide out, so I am not found out being messed up. I still looked great to everyone I was hiding from.

I am not kidding, my friends would see one part of me, and my family saw another. It was a miserable way to live. I could not just be me. I was so terrified if I stopped giving my time and doing for them, who would be around me. I had my immediate family; I did not have anyone else. If I could make a friend I would hold on as tight as I could. As time would go on, I found they were only there for what I could do for them, not for who I was. I would get so hurt by the people around me, but I always did it to myself.

When you say yes, all the time, people start to expect it and demand it. When you say no you start to really see who people really are. My son used to tell me all the time when I got hurt, "mom you do it to yourself, they're not good people, they always expect out of you, and you do it. They never give back". When I eventually listened to what my son said and thought about it, I was able to see that it was true. I had responsibility for the way I was being treated…I allowed it.

I attracted those types of people based on how I felt about myself. I set myself up for crappy friends, and I always expected something different. My son would always tell me, "Don't expect anything out of anyone, because you will always be disappointed." I couldn't believe that at first, but when I got tired of always being let down by my friends, I lowered the expectations dramatically. In hindsight, that response was how I saw myself. I felt I was not deserving of friends who would give back to me. I felt I owed people for being such a fraud of a person anyway. Maybe if I did more for others, finally someone who I was trying to get approval from would see the goodness in me. As you can guess, it never happened. I had to learn to get approval from me. That is all that truly matters, the permission from your own self.

I have always said people are mirrors with eyeballs. When you get angry at someone, or there is something you really can't stand in someone, it is already inside of you. Change you, and you will see something beautiful in people. Your level of friends will go up dramatically.

When you do the work on yourself and make changes, you start to see the person who you have been in others or the work you need to continue to do on yourself. This is something I take very seriously. There are no short cuts either. It can be tough and grueling. When you stick with it, you will start to see your higher purpose in life. You will begin to fall in love with your true self and stop fighting against it.

I would make fun of people who followed the rules, did what they were supposed to, and I would see them succeed. I would get so mad and jealous because I longed to be that person and yet I loathed myself so much I thought I would never get there. So why not tear down what you don't believe you can have. I know, it's terrible, but I am being open so you can see something for yourself. There is some part of us who all do it. Some more than others, but we all can relate.

Not knowing who you are or being afraid to let go of what no longer serves you, it can be scary. We can no longer stay stuck because we are so scared of the unknown. We need to pull up our boots and walk through the baggage of our lives, go through it, and let it all go so we can be our true happy, smart selves.

Saying no will start to become liberating to you when you have nothing to hide from, and you are living in confidence. "Yes" will be a word of the past unless it is something you really want to do.

Rule of thumb: when someone asks you to do something, your response is "yes" without hesitation, and you are excited about it, then GO with YES. However, if someone asks you to do something and you have any kind of uncertainties whatsoever, Say NO Immediately…It's not for you to do. You will thank yourself later.

Realization

It's incredible how so many different situations and experiences we have had in our lives create our perceptions to keep us from living our true potential. When we allow our own understanding of any given situation to take over, we can create the worst life ever. When we get the help, we open our eyes and mind to the possibility we can create the best experience for ourselves.

We can be our own worst enemy, especially if we don't let things go. I did some dumb things in my life. One that plagues me the most is so stupid. I have been carrying it around since I was eighteen years old. I am actually going to take this moment and share it with you.

It's crazy, I don't even want to put it into print because I am so ashamed of it. It is not anything serious. It is a time when I decided I was not a good person and not worthy to receive anything wonderful. Okay, here we go…

I took a job at a gas station, yes, I was for a very brief moment a gas station attendant. I had to take a polygraph test for the job, and go through a little red tape, to be a gas station attendant. It was not a job I was excited about, but a position to help pay the bills. I had to count cigarettes and collect payments for gas. Not that hard.

Well, I did a pretty good job until I got some coaching from the guy who worked second shift about skimming a little money. I was young, naive, and impressionable. I really have never done anything terrible…so why not dabble a little. I had no idea what I was doing.

I was also introduced to pot at the time, and I wanted to get some, but I didn't want to use my own money. I am dying laughing right now as I write this, but I think of this event often. I just have to tell on myself so I can let it finally go. Anyway, I really wanted to get a little bag, so I decided to skim some money from my job. I had no idea how to really do it, so I did this whole thing with buying and returning milk and take a dollar for each transaction. I tried to remember what my coworker said but thank goodness I botched the whole thing. I have never stolen anything in my life. When I got to work the next day, my boss had a meeting with me and gave me a choice of a polygraph test or quit. So, I left and went home. I was so embarrassed and mortified by my behavior. I could not believe one, how stupid I was, but most importantly I took what wasn't mine.

OMG!!! I was terrified when I got home, I had to create this whole story about how bad the job was, how I was asked to clean the disgusting bathrooms, and I couldn't do it. So, I quit. My father was going to go right up to the gas station and talk to my manager. I went into a quick panic of NO I hate that job anyway. I will find something else.

Could you imagine telling your parents, I don't know how to steal, and I got caught? Worst, I wanted to buy pot with it. Not only that, my parents would have had my head on a platter and a beating to boot.

This is a foolish thing I have allowed to plague me for a good portion of my life. I am quite embarrassed, but it's true. It happened, and I feel like a weight has been actually lifted off my shoulders. I just set myself free. It's like holding your breath for years, and now I get to take in a deep breath. What a sigh of relief.

Just a few weeks ago I was shoveling snow and this experience popped in my head yet again. I have been so mortified by my behavior at eighteen. I actually made it more debilitating in my life than it needed to be. This is why I decided to share it with you. Once it's out, it can no longer haunt me.

When you start to realize and put situations into perspective, you begin to give yourself a sense of freedom that you are not used to. I have been carrying that shame for thirty-two years. That is a long time to hold on to something that keeps you stuck. What you resist always persists until you get complete with it. I made myself a horrible, dishonest person with that experience. I felt like I did not deserve anything good to happen to me. I would be punished for my behavior forever. That is what I lived into, I have spent so many years proving to myself I am not a good person, and I do not deserve great things in life. Doing the best, I can with any job I have ever had, just to make up for the gas station job. It was a job I really never wanted, but for the first time with a job, I did not produce my best work. I took what was not mine for something so stupid. Just to let you know, I never bought the pot, it just wasn't worth it. Although, I did learn how people get themselves trapped in the police system when you do something so stupid. I am so grateful to my Angels to have always been looking out for me and thank goodness my boss at the time did not call the police. I think he knew I was a good kid that tried something so dumb.

To even talk about this particular experience has actually liberated me, I am teaching an Angel Writing class, and I am using this specific experience as an example of how my Angels communicate with me through writing.

When you start to realize why you do the things you do in life, you have the opportunity to change or not change. You get to decide how your life is going to go and it puts you in the driver's seat. You are no longer allowing some old story to keep you stuck in your life.

We have all types of patterns of behavior that is influenced by when we are very young. As an adult, different experiences will start to emerge and stop us in our tracks. We are not even really sure what is happening until we start to have destructive behavior.

When you are healing, diving into your life and practicing self-development, all kinds of things may come up. Memories are a considerable part of what comes up. As an adult, the memories are vague but familiar. However, our younger soul always remembers what we try to hide; when it's time to heal we remember and let go.

I just did a healing with a friend of mine who does Healing on a deep Soul level, her name is Elisa Kehler. Elisa is helping me to heal and release all that plagues me from my past. I have always dealt with my weight since I was eleven years old. I have taken diet pills since I was in high school, there really isn't too much in the diet industry I have not done or tried. It has always been exhausting trying to release the weight for it to come right back on. Elisa went into my solar plexus (third Chakra) and saw when I was a child, food that I loved was taken away, or I was forced to eat the stuff I hated. Elisa saw this happening when I was very young, but somehow it made sense to me. The food I loved felt like there was not enough, and I was hungry. What I hated, I had to learn how to eat it without it touching my tongue.

Food has always been a trigger, now that we are healing that pain on the soul level, I can finally release the weight. I am so grateful for this work because what we think is impossible really isn't. When we are ready, the teachers always show up for us as healers.

I can't tell you how many amazing people have been put on my path to help me keep moving forward. I have so many healer friends who have been strategically placed along with psychic mediums as well. I have been able to keep moving forward on my journey to do the great things I do for people.

Anytime I have ever been stuck in my life, I have had an Angel placed before me. It's the most fantastic thing actually to recognize it and receive them. We always have a fair exchange, I give to them, and they give me what I need most at that moment.

I grew up in a life that allowed me to learn more than I could have ever imagined. There was not one thing I would have done differently, because who is in my life today, I can never do without. I have been able to learn what to do as well as what not to do. I have been taught there is always something deeper happening then what is in front of me. I have learned it is okay to be done with a relationship and walk away when it is no longer serving me.

I have had many lessons in my life, and now it is time for me to start enjoying the blessings. That goes for you as well. What is it that you are doing in your life that you don't understand where it's coming from? When you are not afraid to dive into your life to set yourself free and others, great rewards come to you. When you hold on tight, and you are so scared to make a move, and you don't, you just stay stuck with the same old behavior that does not suit you.

When you are afraid of discovering and making moves that is what you should be doing. When you are comfortable in the same old same old, and you say, "well that's just how they are," or worse, "that's just how I am." That means you have resigned yourself and you are no longer trying to be the best version of yourself. I could never imagine not growing and stretching myself, trying something new. Some people can't handle it, but for me, it's a ride I never want to get off of.

Self-Realization is a tool I love using in my life, I am always ready to learn and be my best self. Even when someone says something to me about how I am being, I look at it and change it. I don't get offended. I may get mad inside myself. It is always an opportunity for introspection and growth.

When you can look at your own self from someone else's perspective, you actually show that you are a fantastic person. You confirm that you care more about other people than being right in your behavior. I love that about myself, I will be the first one to tell on myself, I don't want anything holding me back.

Now What?

I have talked about so many facets that keep me stuck, and I am confident you can relate as well. Once we start to really dive into what is happening with us, what do we do with it? How do we motivate ourselves to shift, change and make things happen?

I learned a long time ago I am special. Special in a sense that I know I am here to help people be great in their lives. I am the flashlight shining bright on their greatness so they can discover it themselves as well as my own self. I know the more I forgive, love and accept the more I can change and do great things for myself as well as for others.

My son supports me to continue on this fantastic journey. I want to teach my son there is no giving up, no matter how hard things get, there is always something for us to learn and grow from.

I have always had big dreams for myself. It's a deep burning desire to be bigger than myself, to be kind and loving to myself and everyone around me. Sometimes that is not as easy as it sounds. I spent much time beating myself up and others until I finally decided to be responsible for my own self. I changed the way I see the world and the world sees me.

I have met plenty of people who spend thousands of dollars on becoming successful, but the one thing that stops them in life is their attitude. They are not interested in getting to the root problem of who they are. Either it is too painful for them, or it is too much hard work. What I have learned is that what you resist, it will always persist until you take care of it.

I have also learned in general people are not mean. However, they become mean from their experiences in life. They have made decisions very young that has shaped them into who they are at present until they decide their way of living is no longer serving them.

In my angriest phase in life, I was about twenty-four to twenty-five years of age, when people thought I was mean. I had no idea anyone thought of me other than a hardworking employee. I had gotten feedback from one person in particular who would tell me, I thought I was all that. She said I would walk around like I owned the office and was abrupt, not very approachable. I had no idea people saw me the way. I thought I was friendly and funny. However, they had no idea what was going on in my own personal life. I started a new job, I had trouble in my marriage, I had a sickly young child, and I was barely making it health wise myself. I had so many things I was worried about, it landed right on my face and on my sleeve.

I now see why my co-workers thought of me that way, but I had so much going on in my personal life, I was literally suffocating. I actually had an asthma attack so bad I landed in the emergency room very close to death. My husband at the time left me at the hospital. He felt that the doctors would figure out my problem, so he went home with our son. I found out later, the hospital had to call him, so they could get a priest in for my last rights. I had declined so fast, they had to intubate me so a machine could breathe for me. The next morning, I woke up not breathing on my own, alone in the ICU. I was never more terrified and alone in my whole life. My husband at the time came in around ten thirty in the morning, to see how I was doing. The crazy thing was, he never called my work to let them know what happened and that I was not coming in. Even as I am writing, I have sadness in my heart, tears in my eyes, because no one has ever understood me. I had been alone my whole life at this point, and I knew it was not going to get any better.

Looking back at that time, it was no wonder I was someone who was not approachable or that I was abrupt. I had no family, a husband who kept getting arrested in three different counties. I also had my son as well as myself to take care of. I was tapped out. We never really know why someone is the way they are. They may be sweet and kind people ready to do whatever it takes, but they have so much other heavy stuff going on in their lives. It took everything out of them just to keep going. That was me one hundred percent.

Years later, I had finally had enough and decided to get unmarried from my first husband. That is when my career of self-development started. It took a little while for me to become softer on the outside, but I never quit on myself, and I kept going. I began to realize the world did not revolve around me. I needed to be patient, kind and come from a place of love when dealing with people. I also had to take full responsibility for how my life was going. I needed to make better choices to make my own life great. I can't cry about my life if I am not willing to do anything about it.

It always seems to boggle my mind with people who don't want to change or blame everyone for their own stuff. I have done things in my life I am not proud of, but I see I was young and uneducated in a sense I did not know any better. However, when you grow up, and start to understand different perspectives of what went on. You then need to be responsible for how you respond. Life is all about learning and growing. If you stay stuck, you will lead a miserable life that leaves you feeling empty.

Being fifty years old right now, looking back at a lot of the events that occurred in my life. Some I had zero control over, and the rest, I had chosen the best as I could as I grew. Before I knew any better, I handled myself poorly. Knowing this, I can either continue to punish myself for the rest of my life, or I can use it to my advantage and do great things.

Sometimes we feel so terrible about our behavior, we will get trapped beating ourselves up for a bit. However, when you start to realize different perspectives of what really is happening in a particular event, you will see it's not all about you. Only then will you begin to change your behavior. You will start to realize that everything, no matter what the outcome, has been for your highest good.

Who Cares…Just Do It!

When we realize how everything in our lives has occurred, and we realize everything in hindsight has happened for our highest good, we can start moving forward. We can start taking the action steps in our life. Our dreams we have been longing for starts to have some sort of light shining letting us know we are moving forward from our past.

How amazing is that? We are finally starting to learn the lessons in life, we are getting the experience and the knowledge we need to make our dreams come true. When we see the obstacles in our way, instead of caving and falling back into our puddles, we can rise above and move forward. We even get all giddy when we realize how awesomely smart and powerful, we are. It truly is a fantastic thing.

Here I am, fifty years old, unmarried for the second time finally living on my own. This was not some small task my friends. I never really saw myself living on my own, or unmarried for the second time. I did not think I was really capable of being independent.

I have always tried creating a business for myself but struggled. I knew the corporate world was never really for me. I wanted somehow to help people, but if I was on my own, how would I do that?

My marriage was pretty lifeless. I would complain, cry about how my life was so empty and lonely.

I knew I no longer belonged in that home and I had no idea how I was going to survive without my son being with us if I stayed. He was getting older and just itching to get out. I found out later he stayed as long as he did for me. He did not want to leave me there by myself. I was sick from all the stress. All the strange but very complicated and severe illnesses were hitting me left and right. In fact, the last three years have been all about doctors.

Last February was my last surgery and the last of all my major medical problems. I decided to become unmarried in March, and everything changed after that. When that decision was made, it was as if the skies opened up, the sun came out and has not stopped shining ever since. In fact, everything started falling into place all at once.

You might be asking yourself at this point, why does she keep saying she is unmarried? What does that mean? She said she was divorced but kept referring to being unmarried. Being unmarried is a choice. I am not happy or unhappy about the situation. I am choosing my words powerfully, so I do not continue the negative dialogue to myself. When you choose to be unmarried, you are free from the drama. When you talk about being divorced, everyone gets a painful sinking feeling that leaves you not feeling so great. I chose to be unmarried and live powerfully. I dare the phrase "unmarried" to catch on.

I was able to file for divorce in May when we got our income tax return, and by the end of July, it was all said and done. My friends were able to help me get everything I needed for when I moved out of the house. I was able to purchase my bed and mattress, we separated our belongings, my friends gave me things to furnish my home, and it was unbelievable. It was falling into place so fast, I kept taking the action steps, and my son got nervous for me. I had to keep reassuring him it would be okay.

The only thing holding me back was the fact I had nowhere to go. I wanted to be in my own place by June. Why June? I had made up my mind; that's what I wanted. I needed to get out of the basement and sleep in my own bed. I was desperate for my bed and have a good night sleep. I had gotten a few leads on places, but it never really panned out. I knew deep down; my home was becoming available. I just had to be patient.

It was a beautiful Tuesday late afternoon, four thirty pm to be exact, my phone had an apartment notification for me. I called my best friend, Mary, who is a fantastic real estate agent, and told her we need to see this particular apartment today. The incredible thing about this, it had just gone on the market when I got the notification, we were at the apartment by six pm, and I knew this is where I was going to be living.

You know your life is going just the way it needs to be when it all falls into place all at once.

I gathered all the documents and money I needed, and by Friday the apartment was mine. By Saturday I was completely moved in. It literally took five days from seeing my new place to be settled in. What else was amazing, everything I gathered for myself and from my friends, it was as if everyone was holding my stuff for me from a previous life. It was like I emptied my storage facility that was spread across my friends. Literally, everything in my place all went together as if it was supposed to be that way. It's a miracle, to say the least.

What I have learned is when you start to take action and just do it, no matter what it is; everything falls into place like magic. A significant thing I have noticed, my health is a million times better. I am breathing in more life than I ever had. Asthma is not my primary concern anymore. It's incredible how when you start to really change your life and let go of the emotional baggage you can really take in the air through your lungs. I get up every day grateful for another chance to live. I make my bed and say thank you for being so comfortable, I make my coffee, take care of my kitties, and off I go. When I walk in the door from a long day, I still can't believe I get to live where I live. When I go to bed, I am so thankful for all of it, everything in my life. I would not change a thing.

Isn't that something? I would not change anything, my family, my marriages, all the illness, all the struggles. I would do it all again. I love my life so much. I needed all of what was to make all of what is. It truly is a profound statement. It's TRUE. If one thing ever changed, I would not be the person I am today. I wouldn't be the mother, the friend, the healer, the coach. I wouldn't be me.

 I am so proud of where I come from, that I will do whatever it takes to help others get to where they want to be. I will share my stories, so others feel safe to make the changes in their lives. I will continue to be loving and patient with myself, and I will never be cruel to my person again.

 No matter what it is you want to do you in your life, start taking the action steps to get you there. There is no time limit to where you need to be, and there is nowhere you need to be either. Just do what is right for you and you will start to see your life change. You will begin to attract all that you have been longing for, faster than you could have ever imagined. As I look at my life right here and right now, my heart is beaming with love and joy. There is nothing I regret because I am doing what I love.

 I have now just finished my very first book. I have tears running down my face because these are tears of joy. It does not matter how my writing is received, because I know I am helping at least one person. I am not going to worry whether or not it is liked, because I have never written a book before, and this is how I am doing it. I finally said Who CARES…JUST DO IT!!!

About Rita T. Owen

Rita T. Owen is a Spiritual Coach and Angel Reader. Her passion has always been to help people get out of their own way. She is a firm believer that no matter what you have been through you can live an extraordinary life. Rita can channel messages from the Angels. Her spiritual gifts have allowed her to communicate with the other side to deliver messages to her clients. Rita is an Empath who uses all four of her spiritual senses to help you live powerfully.

She is a Reiki Master, Chios Practitioner, a certified Master Life Coach and Law of Attraction Practitioner. Rita uses her own life experiences to help people see a different perspective in their own lives.

Her website is www.justritarealtalk.com and her email is justrita@justritarealtalk.com – feel free to reach out!

www.ingramcontent.com/pod-product-compliance
Lightning Source LLC
LaVergne TN
LVHW041547070426
835507LV00011B/967